## WOMEN OF FAITH®

# HOPE

## THE ANCHOR FOR YOUR SOUL

THOMAS NELSON PUBLISHERS®

Nashville

Published by Thomas Nelson, Inc., P.O. Box 141000, Nashville, Tennessee, 37214.

Scripture quotations marked (NKJV) are taken from the *Holy Bible, New King James Version*®.
Copyright © 1982 by Thomas Nelson, Inc. All rights reserved.

Scripture quotations marked (KJV) are taken from the *King James Version*.

Scripture quotations marked (NCV) are taken from *The Holy Bible, New Century Version* ®,
Copyright © 1987, 1988, 1991 by Word Publishing, a division of Thomas Nelson, Inc. Used by Permission.

Scripture quotations marked (NLT) are taken from the *Holy Bible, New Living Translation*, Copyright © 1996.
Used by permission of Tyndale House Publishers, Inc., Wheaton, Illinois 60189. All rights reserved.

Scripture quotations marked (NASB) are taken from the *New American Standard Bible*®
© Copyright The Lockman Foundation 1960, 1962, 1963, 1968, 1971, 1972, 1973, 1975, 1977, 1995.
Used by permission. (www.Lockman.org)

Scripture quotations marked (MSG) are taken from *The Message*. Copyright © by Eugene H. Peterson 1993, 1994, 1995.
Used by permission of NavPress Publishing Group.

Scripture quotations marked (TEV) are taken from *The Holy Bible, Today's English Version*—Second Edition.
Copyright © 1992 by American Bible Society. Used by permission.

Scripture quotations marked (NIV) are taken from the *Holy Bible, New International Version*®. Copyright © 1973, 1978,
1984 by International Bible Society. Used by permission of Zondervan Publishing House. All rights reserved.

Copyright © J.B.PHILLIPS 1958, 1960, 1972. THE GOSPELS © Macmillian Publishing Company, a division of
Macmillian, Inc. 1952, 1957. THE YOUNG CHURCH IN ACTION © Macmillian Publishing Company, a division
of Macmillian, Inc. 1955. LETTERS TO YOUNG CHURCHES © Macmillian Publishing Company, a division of
Macmillian, Inc. 1947, 1957. THE BOOK OF REVELATION © Macmillian Publishing Company, a division of
Macmillian, Inc. 1957.

The quotes from Nicole Johnson are taken from her book *Fresh-Brewed Life*, © 2001 by Nicole Johnson.
Used by permission.

Library of Congress Cataloging-in-Publication Data is available.
ISBN 0-7852-5183-9
Printed in United States
1 2 3 4 5 6 7 — 09 08 07 06 05 04

## Theme Verse

*This hope we have as an anchor of the soul,*
*both sure and steadfast.*

Hebrews 6:19 NKJV

# INTRODUCTION

One of the games our family enjoys playing together is Yahtzee! It's a simple game, and even youngsters can join in. One of the greatest appeals to my sons is the tremendous noise it makes. You rattle five dice in a plastic cup, then send them clattering across the tabletop. What a racket! It's a wonderful game to strengthen math skills, so I'm willing to tolerate the accompanying clamor. But, there is one drawback to the game—at least most tactically-inclined competitors would say so. There is very little strategy involved. In essence, Yahtzee! is a game of chance, and the player is at the mercy of the dice. No matter how much you hope that your last roll will turn up one more six, you cannot make those tumbling cubes bend to your will. All the wishing and wanting in the world cannot affect the outcome of your turn. All the planning in the world cannot influence the dice to turn in your favor. Any novice depending upon pure luck can outdo the most skilled player. Still, we cling to hope where there is none. We chant the number we're looking for, or blow onto the dice before tossing them. Even when the odds are against us, we hope against hope that things will work out.

Our lives are a little like that. Our days are filled with unexpected turns. We never know quite what will turn up. We can't control life, and all the wishing and wanting in the world cannot change that fact. So many souls wander around helplessly, shaken by circumstances and rattled by their own reaction to them. They have nothing to hold onto—nothing to trust. Their lives seem a jumble of disappointed strategies, left to the mercy of nebulous fates. For those who have no glimmer of hope, life is a gamble. Many are left to weigh the odds and hope for the best. Their chances of finding unconditional love, peace, contentment, and a happy ending all on their own is slim to none. Yet this is the best chance that the world can hope for—without Jesus.

There is a vast difference between hoping that something will happen—wishing, wanting, and desiring a favorable outcome—and having hope. If we did not have hope—real hope—because of Jesus, we would be inclined to view life as a completely pointless affair. The strong, clear sense of hope in our lives makes all the difference in the world. No matter how dark our day might be, even the barest reminder of our glorious eternal hope is enough to lift the most discouraged heart.

This study is designed to encourage your heart by giving you a clear picture of what true hope is. We will focus in on the questions: What is hope—biblical hope? Why is it ours? Where does it have its Source? What is it we are hoping for? What difference does hope make in our lives? Over the course of the next six weeks, you will discover a hope that gives a reason for rejoicing, the courage to stand unshaken by circumstances, a transformation in our everyday lives, a glimpse of heaven's glories, and the strength to endure until the end. Life is full of ups and downs and unexpected turns, but in the midst of uncertainty, hope is an anchor for your soul.

# Contents

# LESSON 1

# HOPE AND A PROMISE

*"At that time you were without Christ…having no hope and without God"*
Ephesians 2:12 NKJV

## INTRODUCTION BY MARILYN MEBERG

God has called you to be His child, a member of His divine family. One of the riches you inherit as a result of your divine family connection is hope. That hope is because Jesus Himself lives within you. Colossians 1:27 says, " . . . Christ in you, the hope of glory." What does that mean and how does it produce hope?

Quite simply, it means you will never be alone. Jesus is always with you. You will never be abandoned to live out your joys, as well as your sorrows, in isolation. That truth produces hope for every day you are on this earth. That hope goes straight on with you as you enter heaven. How's that for an anchor that's never yanked out of the water?

Here's another hope-producing truth about Jesus in you. When Christ came to earth in the form of a baby, He made Himself like you. After His death and Resurrection, He returned to heaven to help you now be like Him. Because of His indwelling presence, He enables you to be kind when you don't feel like it, patient when you're not, generous when you feel stingy, and gentle when you feel cranky.

Matthew 26:41 encourages you to remember " . . . the spirit is willing, but the flesh is weak." Because Jesus is within you and understands you are weak, you have hope to behave in ways that are like Him.

He knows you can't always be the person you'd like to be. He doesn't blame you, belittle you, or condemn you. He simply helps you.

You are going to have a great trip as you do this lesson on "Hope: The Anchor for Your Soul." I wish I could be there with you sipping tea, sharing, and learning more about you. Incidentally, did you know you can live without chocolate, but you can't live without hope? Enjoy the sail!

## A PEEK AT OUR WEEK

- **Day One:** Without Hope
- **Day Two:** The Hope of His Calling
- **Day Three:** Hope Does Not Disappoint
- **Day Four:** Living Hope
- **Day Five:** The Comfort of the Scriptures

## DAY ONE

# WITHOUT HOPE

*"Those people who are ruled by their sinful selves cannot please God."*
ROMANS 8:8 NCV

Let's say that you hear about a job opening at a local corporation. It sounds interesting, so you make an appointment with their Human Resources department and start getting ready. First thing first—It's been a while since you updated your resume. To make a good impression, you take a special trip to the local office supply store and buy a packet of cream-colored vellum paper. That done, you assess your wardrobe. What to wear? Nothing too somber. Nothing too colorful. You want to look intelligent, capable, and confident—but also communicate an aura of warm approachability. The outfit in hand, you agonize over accessories. Gold or pearls? Patent leather or suede? Heels or flats? While assessing yourself in the mirror, you notice that a trip to the local beauty salon couldn't hurt. You take the time for a manicure and pedicure. A facial brings out the healthy glow in your cheeks. A new cut and some discreet highlighting add drama to your hair. Every possible detail has been thought of. You look impressive!

The morning of your interview, you brush up on your interviewing skills—firm handshake, direct eye contact, genuine smile, clear enunciation. You arrive punctually. You are ready to shine. But halfway through your meeting with the corporate staff, you are stunned to discover that your efforts have been for naught. All of your hopes have been dashed. Despite your impressive resume and your obvious personal charisma, they won't be bringing you on board. You make a fine impression, but you lack the necessary credentials. You are not qualified. You don't meet the criteria. And so, you are sent away.

If you were to ask, most people would say that they hope to go to heaven when they die. They expect to get there because that is where they want to be. It's kind of like declaring your smoking preference— "Would you prefer heaven or hell when you die?" Well, of course paradise sounds more appealing. So they go through their lives trying to make themselves fit in with the heaven-bound crowd. That generally means being good, moral, basically nice people. They cultivate the qualities that they think will soften God's heart toward them, guaranteeing their place in eternal bliss. But no amount of effort on our part will ever gain our entrance into heaven, because effort does not constitute God's criteria for acceptance. Even nice people lack the necessary credentials that the Father requires.

*1. If you had to document your qualifications for acceptance into heaven, what kinds of character qualities do you think would make for an impressive spiritual resume?*

| | | | |
|---|---|---|---|
| ❏ benevolence | ❏ cheerfulness | ❏ sincerity | ❏ likeability |
| ❏ tolerance | ❏ respectfulness | ❏ honesty | ❏ kindness |
| ❏ trustworthiness | ❏ genuineness | ❏ neatness | ❏ selflessness |
| ❏ generosity | ❏ morality | ❏ friendliness | ❏ modesty |
| ❏ loyalty | ❏ good intentions | | |

Wouldn't you be thrilled to document your possession of all these qualities on your resume? Imagine the letters of reference! These traits sum up an ideal woman—niceness personified. The epitome of a good person. The kind of person each of us would want to be. What a noble reputation! And yet none of this impresses God. Even a person with every one of these characteristics has no hope, because these are not the Father's criteria for admission into His presence.

*2.* *That raises the question: What does God want? He tells us in Leviticus 19:2.*

_____

_____

_____

_____

_____

_____

_____

_____

_____

God set the standard for those He would call His own—nothing less than perfection. Holiness is one of God's many attributes. Since God is a holy God, only the holy can stand in His presence.

*3.* *Do we have any hope of meeting that requirement? Read Romans 3:10–12. What is Paul's assessment of our chances?*

_____

_____

_____

_____

_____

_____

The human condition leaves us hopeless, helpless, and hapless in our attempts to spiff up our image. We aren't fooling anyone—especially not God. We're all in the same boat. As Paul so aptly sums it up, "All have sinned and fall short of the glory of God" (Rom. 3:23 NKJV). In fact, God wants us to recognize the fact that we are in a desperate situation. That's one of the reasons that He put the Law in place. It serves as a guide, so that we are aware when we fall short—when we have sinned.

*4. Read Romans 3:19, 20. How does Paul describe the Law's usefulness in regards to sin?*

In Jesus' day, the Pharisees worked very hard at keeping the Law. They led strictly regulated lifestyles, taking great care not to do anything that might compromise their adherence to God's rules. By sheer willpower and some pretty obsessive-compulsive perfectionism, they were able to claim to be righteous before God. Yet when Jesus looked at these very same self-satisfied men, he didn't commend them for their efforts. He didn't congratulate them for setting a good example. He called them a brood of vipers (Matt. 3:7 NKJV)! Even in their efforts to remain above reproach, the Pharisees could not hide their sins from God. Even though they tried very hard to please God, they could not make themselves holy. They, too, were without hope.

> We know that the law's commands are for those who have the law. This stops all excuses and brings the whole world under God's judgment, because no one can be made right with God by following the law. The law only shows us our sin.
>
> Romans 3:19, 20 NCV

## *Did You Know?*

*Because the Pharisees were determined not to break God's command to rest on the Sabbath, they refused to eat any egg that had been laid on a Saturday morning, because the hen had broken the Sabbath in her efforts to lay it.*

*5.* Are there degrees of sin? Are some sins worse than others? Are some sins acceptable under certain circumstances? What does Jesus' own brother declare in James 2:10?

_____

_____

_____

_____

_____

_____

_____

> The law made nothing perfect; on the other hand, there is the bringing in of a better hope, through which we draw near to God.
>
> Hebrews 7:19 NKJV

There are certain things in life that cannot be fudged. The classic example is pregnancy. A woman cannot be "a little bit pregnant." She either is or she isn't. There is no gray area. Another good example would be speeding on the highways and byways. If the speed limit is 55 m.p.h. and you are going 56 m.p.h., then you are speeding. It's pretty cut and dried. In this same way, you can't be just a little bit sinful. With God, it's all or nothing. You are either sinful or you are not. And we are. In fact, we are doomed to face the consequences of our sins. "The law brings about wrath" (Rom. 4:15 NKJV), and "the wages of sin is death" (Rom. 6:23 NKJV). That's why we all begin in such desperate circumstances—"without hope." There is nothing we can do to redeem ourselves.

*6.* Such was our dilemma when God set about to rescue us. See how the tables begin to turn by reading Hebrews 7:19. What has God brought to us?

_____

_____

That "better hope" that has been provided is Jesus Christ. Without Him, we wouldn't have a thread of hope to cling to. Our dependence upon Christ for salvation is the only criteria that God will accept. That's the only qualification He's looking for on our resumes. Only when we belong to Jesus,

## PRAYING GOD'S PROMISES

In order to close this day's lesson, I'd like to invite you to turn one precious passage of Scripture into your own heartfelt prayer. By way of example, join me in this prayer based on Romans 15:8–13:

*Heavenly Father, I cannot say enough how grateful I am that you sent Jesus Christ. He brought the truth. He brought life. He fulfilled the promises that You had made to men. I glorify You for Your mercy. I sing about Your name. I will join all of Your people in rejoicing over You. You have given me hope. O, God of hope, fill me with all joy. Fill my life with peace because I believe in You. By the power of Your Holy Spirit, make me to abound in hope more each day. Amen.*

**Now it's your turn.** Personalize Ephesians 1:11–14, which is printed in the margin, by making it your prayer today.

*In Christ we were chosen to be God's people, because from the very beginning God had decided this in keeping with his plan. And he is the One who makes everything agree with what he decides and wants. We are the first people who hoped in Christ, and we were chosen so that we would bring praise to God's glory. So it is with you. When you heard the true teaching—the Good News about your salvation—you believed in Christ. And in Christ, God put his special mark of ownership on you by giving you the Holy Spirit that he had promised. That Holy Spirit is the guarantee that we will receive what God promised for his people until God gives full freedom to those who are his—to bring praise to God's glory.*

Ephesians 1:11–14 NCV

## DAY TWO

# THE HOPE OF HIS CALLING

*"The eyes of your understanding being enlightened;*
*that you may know what is the hope of His calling."*
Ephesians 1:18 NKJV

In every life, there are turning points. Those times when one thing ends, so that something brand new can begin. It's becoming a "big girl," and ditching your diapers for a pretty pair of pink panties. It's stepping up into the big yellow school bus, to be carried off for your first day of kindergarten. It's getting your first period. It's getting your driver's license. It's getting your high school diploma, your letter of acceptance to the college of your choice, your first job. It's the "I do" you pledge before the altar. It's the doctor's jubilant proclamation, "It's a boy!" Those experiences are defining moments, and with each, a woman becomes something that she had not been before. Yet none of these can compare to the turning point that occurs when a woman finds Jesus.

It's like that familiar phrase from the hymn "Amazing Grace"— "I once was lost, but now I'm found; was blind, but now I see." At the moment when a soul discovers its Savior, it can never be the same. What once was, is no more, and what you become is something altogether new. Today's lesson celebrates the dawning of hope in the life of a believer. Hope that begins with His calling.

*1. The Scriptures condemn us all—we are sinners. But because of Jesus, we have hope. "The Scripture confined all under sin, that the promise by faith in Jesus Christ might be given to those who believe" (Gal. 3:22 NKJV). Look at the following verses. Each has a before and an after—once we were that, but now we are this. For each passage, write down the before and the after.*

| | BEFORE | AFTER |
|---|---|---|
| **Romans 3:28** | | |
| **Romans 8:3** | | |
| **Romans 8:4** | | |
| **Ephesians 2:13** | | |
| **Ephesians 5:8** | | |
| **1 Peter 2:10** | | |

All of this comes about because of God's magnificent plan to give sinners hope. "His name will be the hope of all the world" (Matt. 12:21 NLT). He sent Jesus to die on our behalf, to pay our sin debt and clothe us in His righteousness. "If you confess with your mouth the Lord Jesus and believe in your heart that God has raised Him from the dead, you will be saved" (Rom. 10:9 NKJV). Hope comes to those who believe. "Believe on the Lord Jesus Christ, and you will be saved" (Acts 16:31 NKJV). When we believe, God rejoices. That is exactly what He has been waiting for. In fact, Jesus tells us that all of heaven joins in His pleasure. "There is joy in the presence of the angels of God over one sinner who repents" (Luke 15:10 NKJV). In order to open our eyes to the truth of His love and grace, God woos us—calling to our hearts.

*God had special plans for me and set me apart for his work even before I was born. He called me through his grace.*

Galatians 1:15 NCV

*2. Paul often refers to the Heavenly Father as the God who calls us (Gal. 5:8; 1 Thess. 2:12; 5:24). Look at the following Scriptures. What do they tell us about the God who has called to you?*

● When was Isaiah called by God, according to Isaiah 49:1?

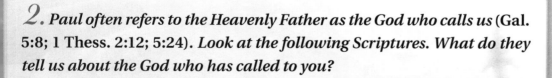

● Why did God call Paul, according to Galatians 1:15?

_____

_____

● What was God's special plan for Paul, according to Romans 1:1?

_____

_____

● How should God's calling affect our lives, according to Ephesians 4:1?

_____

_____

Hope is ours because we have been called. The very word used in the New Testament for church means "those who have been called out." In 1 Corinthians, Paul refers to the believers as "called ones." We are the called. What's more, we are called for a purpose. Paul says we are called to salvation, holiness, and faith (2 Thess. 2:17), we are called to fellowship (1 Thess. 1:12). And, the writer of Hebrews tells us that we are called to an eternal inheritance (Heb. 9:15).

*3. Jesus describes the greatest kind of love for us in John 15:13: "Greater love has no one than this, than to lay down one's life for his friends" (NKJV). How has God extended that very love toward us, and more so, according to Romans 5:6–8?*

_____

_____

_____

_____

_____

God loves us with a love that is greater than we can fathom. Paul prayed, "that you and all God's holy people will have the power to understand the greatness of Christ's love—how wide and how long and how high and how deep" (Eph. 3:18 NCV). And because we are loved, our hearts respond to His. "We loved Him because He first loved us" (1 John 4:19 NKJV). We long to know God, and to see Him someday face to face. That is the dearest hope in our heart of hearts. And so, we are compelled to follow after Him, and to search Him out. When God calls to us, we recognize and respond to His calling.

*4.* *God loves for His children to follow closely after Him. He has laid out the path before us, provided a perfect example for us to emulate, and even urges us along the way.*

___ Psalm 16:11          a. God will show you the path of life.

___ Isaiah 30:21          b. We should follow in Jesus' steps.

___ John 12:26           c. God's guidance will be as clear as a whisper in our ears.

___ 1 Peter 2:21          d. Anyone who serves Jesus follows Him.

*5.* *When we cannot quite see our way, God asks us to seek Him. "I love those who love Me, and those who seek Me diligently will find me"* (Prov. 8:17 NKJV). *Look up these verses that describe our efforts to find the Lord:*

• What will happen if we seek the Lord, according to Deuteronomy 5:29?

- What attitude should we take in seeking after God, according to Jeremiah 29:13?

_____

_____

- Where is God all the while we are pursuing Him, according to Acts 17:27?

_____

_____

God has called to you in order to give you a hope. When your heart responds to His and you believe, you become a new creature. At that point, God's gifts to you are many and varied, but one of those precious gifts is the gift of hope. It is a hope for today. It is a hope for tomorrow. It is a living hope.

### PRAYING GOD'S PROMISES

Today's Scripture prayer is a celebration of the gift of hope that becomes ours when we believe. Join me as we pray, inspired by Paul's words, recorded for us in Acts 17:24–28.

_Father God, You are the ruler of heaven and earth. You made the whole world and everything in it. You have given us life and breath. We try to thank You for our lives in our own way, but nothing we attempt will ever be enough. Our words do not begin to do You justice. Lord, we seek You. We are stretching out our hands, trying to find You. Teach us that You are never far from us. Without Your constant touch, we could not live or move—we would not even exist. And if that was not enough, You have gone even further, by giving us a place in Your family—by making us Your children. Thank You, God! Amen._

We have been called by God. We have heard the Spirit's beckoning. Jesus likened our sensitivity to His call to that of sheep, who know their own Shepherd's voice amidst the din and clamor of other calls and bleating neighbors. "My sheep hear My voice, and I know them, and they follow Me" (John 10:27 NKJV). Take a few minutes to compose a prayer using three Bible verses about following our Lord. They are printed in the margin here.

*You will show me the way of life, granting me the joy of your presence and the pleasures of living with you forever.*

Psalm 16:11 NLT

*If any of you wants to serve me, then follow me. Then you'll be where I am, ready to serve at a moment's notice. The Father will honor and reward anyone who serves me.*

John 12:26 MSG

*Your ears shall hear a word behind you, saying, "This is the way, walk in it," Whenever you turn to the right hand Or whenever you turn to the left.*

Isaiah 30:21 NKJV

## DAY THREE

# HOPE DOES NOT DISAPPOINT

*"Now hope does not disappoint, because the love of God has been poured out in our hearts by the Holy Spirit who was given to us."*
Romans 5:5 NKJV

Have you ever hosted a potluck supper? Some areas call them covered-dish suppers. One church I visited said there wasn't such a thing as luck, so they called their potluck suppers "pot providences." Another church concerned with luck's extra biblical nature called their suppers "pot blessings." Whatever you might call these gatherings, the host provides a place to meet, and the guests all bring a dish to share. You never know quite what the menu will be—lasagna, sloppy joes, green bean casserole, taco salad, or banana cream pie. It's a real smorgasbord. When the invitation goes out, we clear off our counters and dining room table, and wait to see what comes. As minutes tick by, pangs of nervousness creep in, and we begin to have questions. Did everyone get the invitation? Did we get the date and time right? What if our guests arrive, but none of them understood that they were supposed to bring the food? What if everyone brings baked beans? Will there be enough variety? Will there be enough? What if all our hopes for the evening only end in disappointment? Just as we're beginning to think this wasn't such a good idea, there's a knock at the door. Our guests bustle out of their coats and into our kitchen, laden with casseroles, crock pots, Jell-O™ salads, and Bundt cakes. Our home is alive with laughter and fellowship and abundance.

Inviting Jesus into our hearts can be something like inviting God to a potluck supper. We have nothing to offer but the meeting place in our heart. Our cupboards are bare. We mentally pace back and forth, dismayed by our lack of something to offer such an honored Guest. Unsure what to expect, we decide to invite Him in. Yet sometimes we worry about what He'll be bringing with Him. Questions plague us. What if He wants me to be a missionary—to Africa? Will there be a long list of rules to follow? Can He really forgive my sins? Will I be disappointed? Will He really be all I need? Will He be enough? Then Jesus knocks on the door to our hearts, and we open it up to Him. He comes in, and He does not come empty-handed. Though we were dressed in rags, He clothes us in robes of righteousness. Though the table was empty, He placed there the Bread of Life. Though our pitcher was empty, He filled it with living water. Though we were alone, He tells us that He has come to stay. We invite Him in, and He sits down and dines with us (Rev. 3:20). Though we were in a hopeless state, Jesus proved Himself to be an abundant Source of life, fellowship, and hope.

*1.* **If we are honest with ourselves, we might admit that we've wondered if Jesus would be enough—even if everything else was taken away. We have hope, but is hope enough to live for?**

- What is David's attitude about God's enough-ness in Psalm 16:5?

- Some days we aren't sure we can keep going. The task is so big, and we are so small. What is Paul's answer to that dilemma in 2 Corinthians 12:9?

- What does God supply, according to Philippians 4:19?

*The Lord is all I need.*
*He takes care of me.*

Psalm 16:5 NCV

- What does Colossians 2:10 tell us we can be in Christ?

We sing "All to Jesus I surrender," "Jesus is my all," "Thou O Christ art all I want . . .More than all in Thee I find," "Nothing satisfies like Jesus," and "He's all I need," but can that really be true? Indeed it can. Indeed He can. Sometimes, I think we worry that accepting Jesus as our all in all means that we will be living with nothing else. We balk at the idea of letting someone else decide what we need. But God doesn't save us in order to take things away from us.

*2. Our God is not stingy. He doesn't withhold things from those whose hope is in Him. Have you ever considered just how much the Lord provides for us?*

- What does David say God gives to the righteous in Psalm 84:11?

- What does Jesus assure His disciples about God's provisions in Matthew 7:11?

- Why does God give, according to Jesus' own words in Luke 12:32?

- What does James remind us about the good gifts we receive in James 1:17?

God gives us the thing we most need—Himself. We in turn give Him what we have—ourselves. That includes our possessions, our abilities, our time, our spiritual gifts, everything. God doesn't take these things away from us, but He asks us to use them for His glory. He comes to us, offering grace and hope and power and love. Out of love and obedience, we live for God, trusting Him to provide what we need. We have been given all the spiritual resources we need.

Colossians 2:10 says that we are complete in Him. The word for complete in this verse is best translated "fullness," and the tense of the verb tells us that God is the one making it happen—"you have been made full in Christ." Full of what? Full of Jesus. Christ in us. The context in that Colossians passage finds Paul reassuring the church that they don't need to worry about all the philosophies and teachings that run rampant in their society. All they needed was Jesus, plain and simple. In our union with Him, our spiritual needs are met—fully. We have been made full in Him. Or you could say, we have been made full *of Him*.

*The Lord takes pleasure in those who fear Him, In those who hope in His mercy.*

Psalm 147:11 NKJV

*3. So what kinds of things can we hope for when we are depending on God?*

- What does the psalmist hope for in Psalm 147:11?

_____

_____

- What does Solomon say is the hope of the righteous in Proverbs 10:28?

_____

_____

- What does Jeremiah say to the Lord in Jeremiah 17:17?

_____

_____

Jesus brings hope into our hearts. Hope for love. Hope for mercy. Hope for grace. Hope for forgiveness. Hope for help. Hope for change. Hope for purpose. Hope for freedom from sin's power. Hope for strength to face each day. Hope for friendship. Hope for a fresh start. Hope for answered prayers. Hope for patience. Hope for joy. Hope for the future.

*4. The hope Jesus brings to our hearts does not come empty-handed. What does Paul say accompanies the hope of God's calling in Ephesians 1:18, 19?*

Ephesians is a wonderful epistle for reveling in the riches that are ours through Christ. When Jesus becomes our all, we are not left paupers in the world. His gifts may not be monetary ones, but Paul assures us that they are riches indeed. Paul's prayer for us is that our eyes would be opened enough to grasp just how precious our hope really is. Just look at Ephesians 1:18, 19 and the gifts Paul places alongside hope—glory, inheritance, and exceedingly great power. Other translations use descriptions like "wonderful future" (NLT), "rich and glorious inheritance"(NLT), "rich and glorious blessings" (NCV), and speak of the "incredible greatness" (NLT), and the "surpassing greatness of His power" (NASB) that is available to us.

*5. These are all good hopes, but think for a minute. When we talk about "hope," what exactly are we hoping for? What does it all boil down to? Paul sums it up for us in Titus 1:2.*

**6.** In Colossians 1:27, Paul ties two phrases together. It's like saying this **will bring about** this. Or this **equals** this. **What does Paul say comes of "Christ in you"?**

> *Your eyes focused and clear, so that you can see exactly what it is he is calling you to do, grasp the immensity of this glorious way of life he has for Christians. Oh, the utter extravagance of his work in us who trust him— endless energy, boundless strength!*
>
> Ephesians 1:18, 19 MSG

**7.** We all have hopes. When we become believers, new hopes open up to us that we never had before. What is **the hope** of David's life? Not just any old hope, but **the** hope, according to **Psalm 17:15**?

*For this reason I bow my knees to the Father of our Lord Jesus Christ, from whom the whole family in heaven and earth is named, that He would grant you, according to the riches of His glory, to be strengthened with might through His Spirit in the inner man, that Christ may dwell in your hearts through faith; that you, being rooted and grounded in love, may be able to comprehend with all the saints what is the width and length and depth and height—to know the love of Christ which passes knowledge; that you may be filled with all the fullness of God.*

Ephesians 3:14–19 NKJV

Paul knew the importance of hope, and he knew the One in which all our hope rests. If it were not for Jesus, our hopes would all die. If it were not for hope, we would die. But Paul wrote with confidence, "Paul, an apostle of Jesus Christ, by the commandment of God our Savior and the Lord Jesus Christ, our hope" (1 Tim. 1:1 NKJV). Because of Jesus, our hope is alive.

## PRAYING GOD'S PROMISES

Today, our Scripture prayer is based upon Paul's words on hope from Romans 5:1–5.

*Faithful Father, thank You for giving us a hope that can never disappoint. Thank You for Jesus, for without Him, we would be hopelessly lost. Through Him we have peace with You. Through Him we have found grace. Now our hearts are rejoicing, because we have the hope of life, of glory, of seeing You. Teach me to continue to rejoice, even when circumstances frustrate me. Give me the strength I need to persevere, one day at a time. Remind me that the difficulties I face produce character in me. Through Your Spirit, sharpen my awareness of hope, and make it enough to live for. Pour Your great love over my heart, and show me that You are all I will ever need. Amen.*

**Now it's your turn.** Read slowly through the selected passage from Ephesians in the margin. It is a prayer of Paul's which beautifully expresses just a few of the riches that are ours from our Heavenly Father. Take a little time to make this passage your own prayer.

# DAY FOUR

## LIVING HOPE

*"Blessed be the God and Father of our Lord Jesus Christ, who according to His abundant mercy has begotten us again to a living hope through the resurrection of Jesus Christ from the dead."*

1 Peter 1:3 NKJV

Peter says that through Jesus, we have a living hope. What is the difference between a hope that is living and a hope that is dead? Hopeless hopes do not have any basis in reality. They are pipe dreams or castles in the air that we have built up for ourselves. They depend upon some unlikely string of circumstances. As children, we had high hopes. "I wish I could have a pony." (Never mind the fact that you lived in an apartment.) "I wish I could win an Olympic gold medal." (Never mind the years of dedicated practice required.) "I wish I could be an astronaut." (Never mind the years of study and the strict selection process.) The personal cost involved in these aspirations never occurred to us. Even as adults, we tend to want to wish away our problems. "I wish I could win the lottery." (Never mind the odds against us.) "I wish I were young again." (Never mind the impossibility of turning back the years.) These hopes and wishes would require a miracle to bring them about. They are hopes with no hope of ever coming to pass.

Are believers clinging to hope where there is none? No indeed! Our hopes are not dead. We have a living hope. A living hope is a hope we can depend upon coming to pass. A living hope is a hope that is sure to be realized someday—guaranteed.

*1.* **Peter calls our hope a "living hope" (1 Pet. 1:3). What makes it live, according to 1 Peter 1:21?**

_____

_____

_____

_____

_____

_____

> *Through Christ you have come to trust in God. And because God raised Christ from the dead and gave him great glory, your faith and hope can be placed confidently in God.*
>
> 1 Peter 1:20, 21 NLT

It's quite simple really. Our hope is alive because Jesus is alive. We will live because He lives. We have a living hope because we serve a living Lord. This is so foundational to the Christian faith that Paul took the time to spell it out for us.

*2.* **Let's take a look at 1 Corinthians 15:13–19. Paul makes several logical "if . . . then" statements. Let's list them below:**

IF there is no resurrection of the dead (v. 13),

THEN _____

IF Jesus is not risen (v. 14),

THEN _____

IF our preaching is empty (v. 14),

THEN _____

IF Christ is not risen (v. 17),

THEN _____

IF believers are still in their sins (v. 18),

THEN _____

IF hope in Christ is not for eternal life (v. 19),

THEN _____

We have hope—hope of glory. Our hope is living because we will see it come to pass someday. Jesus is our source of hope. Our living hope depends on a living Lord.

*3. Look at these different Scriptures. Some of them point to the fact that Jesus our Savior is alive. But He's not the only one!*

| | |
|---|---|
| ___ Matthew 16:16 | a. Adam became a living being. |
| ___ John 6:51 | b. God's Word is living and powerful. |
| ___ John 7:38 | c. We trust in a living God. |
| ___ Romans 12:1 | d. Jesus is the living bread. |
| ___ 1 Corinthians 15:45 | e. We are made alive by the Spirit. |
| ___ 1 Timothy 6:17 | f. Jesus is the Son of the living God. |
| ___ Hebrews 4:12 | g. We can present ourselves as living sacrifices. |
| ___ 1 Peter 3:18 | h. Rivers of living water flow from believers' hearts. |

Peter tells us of our living hope. The Greek word used in the New Testament for hope can be translated "expectancy," and the word for living means just that, "living." But from Peter's perspective, our living hope is not the opposite of dead hope. We tend to think of opposites more than they did—must be our Sesame Street training. Our living hope is the opposite of the hopeless hope that the world has. Theirs is empty, meaningless—much worse than a hope that has died. They never had a hope in the first place. We, on the other hand, have a living, vibrant hope. It gives us meaning, keeps us full. It is vital, energetic, thriving, dynamic.

*4. Our hope did not come without its cost. Jesus had to die in order for us to live. He paid the price for our redemption. Galatians 3:13, 14 says that Jesus redeemed us so that "we might receive the promise of the Spirit through faith" (NKJV). Where does that leave us? How does Paul describe our obligation in 1 Corinthians 6:20?*

Redeemed. Not a word we use much, outside of church and the grocery store. We redeem coupons in order to lower the price of a product at the checkout counter. But that practice has little if anything to do with God's plan of redemption. In Christian circles, we talk about redeeming the time (Eph. 5:16; Col. 4:5) and being a redeemed people. We sing songs like, "Redeemed how I love to proclaim it, redeemed by the blood of the Lamb!" But redeemed is one of those Christian-ese, church jargon-y terms. We're used to hearing it, but many of us would be hard-put to define it!

Simply put, redeemed means bought. We have been purchased. We belong to God. Body and soul. Lock, stock, and barrel. He holds the deed. The title's in His name. He owns us. But wait. There is a nuance in the original language here. The Greek word for redeemed means "something that has been purchased in order to be set free or to be made whole." Christ's blood redeems us by setting us free from the debt of sin. Paul often encourages us to live in such a way that is worthy of the great price paid on our behalf. "You were bought at a price; therefore glorify God in your body and in your spirit, which are God's" (1 Cor. 6:20 NKJV).

## Did You Know?

*When a Jewish woman gave birth to her first son, she knew she'd be headed up the steps to the temple in forty days in order to redeem him. You see, God had put His "dibbs" on every firstborn male. "They belong to me" (cf. Ex. 13:2, 12). Parents had to bring a sacrifice to the priests in order to "buy back" their son from the Lord. This is why we find Joseph and Mary at the temple with their pair of doves to redeem baby Jesus, Mary's firstborn Son.*

*5. Have you ever gone through a section of the Bible and tried to pick it apart so that you could better understand what it was saying? Let's walk through a passage in 1 Peter together. First of all, read through the whole paragraph—1 Peter 1:13–23. Then answer these questions:*

- According to verse 13, on what does our hope rest?

- How are we to behave ourselves, according to verse 14?

- Why, according to verses 15 and 16?

- Who is Peter talking to in verse 17?

*13 Therefore gird up the loins of your mind, be sober, and rest your hope fully upon the grace that is to be brought to you at the revelation of Jesus Christ; 14 as obedient children, not conforming yourselves to the former lusts, as in your ignorance; 15 but as He who called you is holy, you also be holy in all your conduct, 16 because it is written, "Be holy, for I am holy." 17 And if you call on the Father, who without partiality judges according to each one's work, conduct yourselves throughout the time of your stay here in fear; 18 knowing that you were not redeemed with corruptible things, like silver or gold, from your aimless conduct received by tradition from your fathers, 19 but with the precious blood of Christ, as of a lamb without blemish and without spot.*

*1 Peter 1:13–19 NKJV*

*²⁰ He indeed was foreordained before the foundation of the world, but was manifest in these last times for you ²¹ who through Him believe in God, who raised Him from the dead and gave Him glory, so that your faith and hope are in God. ²² Since you have purified your souls in obeying the truth through the Spirit in sincere love of the brethren, love one another fervently with a pure heart, ²³ having been born again, not of corruptible seed but incorruptible, through the word of God which lives and abides forever.*

1 Peter 1:20–23 NKJV

- How should we conduct ourselves, according to verse 17?

- What was the cost of our redemption, according to verse 19?

- Who did Jesus come for, according to verse 20?

- What did God do for Jesus in verse 21?

- Why (or "so that"), according to verse 21?

- Because of all this ("since"), we should do what, according to verse 22?

- And how was the incorruptible seed planted, according to verse 23?

God planned for our redemption even before the foundation of the world, so that even before sin entered the picture, a way for salvation had been made. Hope did not come cheaply. Peter's reminder is stern. He watched Jesus die. He saw how much Christ was made to suffer. Peter urges us not to forget, the blood of Christ is precious, and we should never take its cost lightly. Live in a manner worthy of the One whose name you claim. Peter says to live a life of holiness, in godly fear, purified by obedience, and characterized by sincere love from a pure heart.

*6. Those who are saved by God belong to Him. Paul refers to "the God to whom I belong and whom I serve" (Acts 27:23 NKJV). And even Jesus tells His disciples to show kindness "because you belong to Christ" (Mark 9:41 NKJV). What do these verses say about those who belong to God?*

- What does Paul say changes when we come to Christ, according to 2 Corinthians 5:15?

- What does Paul say he has died to in Galatians 2:19?

- What should we now live for, according to 1 Peter 2:24?

Our hope is secure because of the One on which it depends. We serve a living God. Jesus is the living Word. The Word of God is living and powerful. God created us to be living beings, but sin brought death. Through Jesus' death, we were given hope—a living hope. Our hope is for eternal life. Until our hope is realized, we live for the One who saved us. Our lives are a living sacrifice. We live in the joy and peace that come from abounding hope.

*Some people, by always continuing to do good, live for God's glory, for honor, and for life that has no end. God will give them life forever.*

Romans 2:7 NCV

*So brothers and sisters, since God has shown us great mercy, I beg you to offer your lives as a living sacrifice to him. Your offering must be only for God and pleasing to him, which is the spiritual way for you to worship. Do not change yourselves to be like the people of this world, but be changed within by a new way of thinking. Then you will be able to decide what God wants for you; you will know what is good and pleasing to him and what is perfect.*

Romans 12:1, 2 NCV

## PRAYING GOD'S PROMISES

First Corinthians 15 is a good passage on which to base a prayer of thanksgiving. Paul is so clear in explaining the basis for our hope. Pray with me this adaptation of 1 Corinthians 15:13–19:

*Giver of Hope, Thank You for showing us how much our lives depend upon You. We thank You for Your Son's sacrifice. We are awed by the power You displayed in raising Him from the dead. We know that if You were able to raise up Jesus, we too can be raised to eternal life. Thank You for the forgiveness from sin that we enjoy because Jesus lives. We trust You, God. Our faith is strong because Your faithfulness is unfailing. No one can call our faith futile. No one can call our lives pitiable. Our hope lives! We depend upon You to bring our hope to pass, and long for the day when we will see You face to face. Amen.*

**Now it is your turn.** We talked a lot today about the life that is ours because of Jesus. But we also touched on the fact that our life belongs to God because of Jesus. Our living hope results in a life lived for God—a living sacrifice. Take a little time to ponder how the adjacent verses affect your life, then journal your prayer here.

## DAY FIVE

# THE COMFORT OF THE SCRIPTURES

*"Whatever things were written before were written for our learning, that we through the patience and comfort of the Scriptures might have hope."*

Romans 15:4 NKJV

We talk a lot about promises. A warm day in March holds the promise of spring. A gray day with lowering clouds holds the promise of rain. A promising youngster is quick-witted and polite. Promising news hints at good things to come. We say, "A promise is a promise," or, "I can't make any promises." We might promise to give something our best effort. We promise ourselves that we'll do better the next time. People who keep their promises are called "as good as their word," and it is a high compliment to call someone a "man of his word." Trust is often based on someone's ability to keep promises. Too many people make promises lightly and then break them without regret. These are piecrust promises—easily made, easily broken.

God has promised us hope. He says that it is ours, and we can trust His Word. How do we know that we have hope? The God who is as good as His word gave us His Word, and that is where we turn for reassurance. "Such things were written in the Scriptures long ago to teach us. They give us hope and encouragement as we wait patiently for God's promises" (Rom. 15:4 NLT). When it comes to bolstering our hope, there is no greater source of comfort than the Scriptures.

*1.* **Why does John say that he wrote down his gospel, according to John 20:31?**

*2.* **What you hold in your hands is pretty amazing. Your Bible was written by many men over the course of many centuries, and yet its message comes right from God. How does Peter describe this miracle in 2 Peter 1:21?**

> All Scripture is given by inspiration of God, and is profitable for doctrine, for reproof, for correction, for instruction in righteousness, that the man of God may be complete, thoroughly equipped for every good work.
>
> 2 Timothy 3:16, 17 NKJV

*3.* **If you want to make sure you've got the real story, the saying goes that you need to get it straight from the horse's mouth. If you are going to rely on God's Word, basing your life on its promises, isn't it a comfort to know that God was directing the writers of Scripture? How does 2 Timothy 3:16, 17 put it?**

Our faith depends heavily on our presupposition that what the Bible says is true.

Do you know what He's said? Do you know what He's promised? Let's take a sampling from the psalms. David wasn't shy about telling God how much He meant to him. In fact, being the poetic soul that he was, David expressed his love for God in beautiful ways. Let's take a look at all the ways David told God that he knew how much He had done and was doing in his life.

*4. David spoke to God in the psalms, often using the phrase, "You are my. . ." "You are my Lord" (Ps. 16:2), "You are my God (Ps. 31:14), "You are my King" (Ps. 44:4). Look up each of these verses and fill in the blank. "You are my. . ." what?*

- Psalm 31:3    You are my _____

- Psalm 31:4    You are my _____

- Psalm 32:7    You are my _____

- Psalm 40:17   You are my _____

- Psalm 71:5    You are my _____

- Psalm 71:7    You are my _____

- Psalm 119:5   You are my _____

## Did You Know?

*In the Old Testament, portion is often used when talking about dividing up land, food, and the spoils of war. David says to God, "You are my portion." He was dependant on the Lord, not on his possessions. He was saying, "God, You are everything I need." Interestingly enough, in the New Testament, Jesus says to Martha that Mary had chosen (literally) the "good portion" (Luke 10:42). Mary chose God. He was her all in all. God was her portion, and it was good. Martha needed some of that portion.*

Does that encourage you? It should. If God was all that for David, doesn't it make sense that He could be all that to you? Sometimes, we don't expect much from God simply because we do not know what He can do. God reveals Himself to us through His Word. He gives us a glimpse of who He is, and He lets us know what He has promised to do. He tells us what He has done, He tells us why He did it, He tells us what we must do, He tells us how He will reward us, He tells us His plans, He shows us the outcome. It's all right there on the pages of our Bibles, and it's all about God!

*5. So is it good enough to read through the Bible once? twice? If the Scriptures are our source of hope and comfort, why limit ourselves? Read. Read again. Read voraciously, passionately, systematically, repeatedly, steadily, thoughtfully. Even if we know the truth, we can all use reminders. What kind of value did Peter put on reminders, according to 2 Peter 1:12–15?*

Reminders. We all need them. A bit of string tied around your finger, a list on the refrigerator, a note by the front door, Post-it™ notes everywhere. Some things come in with built-in reminders. Babies cry when they're hungry. Puppies whimper when they need to go out. Lights flash on our dashboard when the car needs oil, gas, or windshield washing fluid. God has His own reminders for us. Every spring, when the earth stirs with new life. Every sunrise, every star, every snowflake, every breath, every heartbeat. It all points us to the God who created us and sustains us.

*6. Even Paul knew the value of a good reminder! What does he say in Philippians 3:1?*

We are to love God with all our heart and with all our soul, with all our mind and with all our strength. This is the part where your mind comes in. Use your head, ladies. Go to God's Word and find out what He has said—about Himself, about His promises to you, about the hope

He extends to you. Your Bible is God's gift to you. Something tangible, something you can hold in your hands. Open that book. Read those pages. Study it. Mull it over. Apply it. Commit those precious words to heart. Fix them in your minds and trust them. They are the words of hope. They are words of life.

## PRAYING GOD'S PROMISES

When it comes to what the Bible says about itself, there is no greater ode to the Scriptures than the one found in Psalm 119. One hundred seventy-six verses long, and hardly a verse goes by without the psalmist talking about God's Word. Today's prayer is drawn from a smattering of verses taken from the 119th Psalm.

*Keeper of Promises, I thank You for Your Word. Your promises have given me something to hope for. Open my eyes, so that I can see all of the wondrous things in Your Word. I will seek You there with all my heart. I will meditate on Your wonderful works. I will delight in the Word because I have come to love it. I believe Your Word is true. It comforts me. It gives me life. I live to keep Your Word. Uphold me as I follow You. Amen.*

***Now it's your turn.*** We'll take a look at a few verses from John that talk about the words of Jesus. When Job was suffering, he chided his so-called friends, saying, "How then can you comfort me with empty words?" (Job 21:34 NKJV). But we have the comfort of the Scriptures, and the words we find in the Word are not empty. Ponder over what the gospel says about the words of Christ, then blend them into a prayer below.

*Most assuredly, I say to you, he who hears My word and believes in Him who sent Me has everlasting life, and shall not come into judgment, but has passed from death into life.*

John 5:24 NKJV

*It is the Spirit who gives life; the flesh profits nothing. The words that I speak to you are spirit, and they are life.*

John 6:63 NKJV

*But Simon Peter answered Him, "Lord, to whom shall we go? You have the words of eternal life."*

John 6:68 NKJV

## Conclusion

Our hope is two-fold—a hope and a promise. As believers, as children of God, we have a living hope. No longer trapped in a hopeless existence, we are able to look on the bright side, even though we still live in a sin-filled world. "The path of the just is as the shining light that shines more and more into the perfect day. The way of the wicked is darkness; they do not know at what they stumble across" (Prov. 4:18, 19 NKJV). We aren't stumbling around in darkness anymore, because we walk in hope! We have Jesus, and He is enough. We have God, and He is our good portion. This is a blessing from God—hope for each day. What's more, we have a future hope that has been promised to us—the hope of Jesus' return for those who belong to Him. The hope of waking in glory and seeing our Savior face to face. The hope of eternal life. Because of Jesus, we have an inheritance awaiting us in heaven.

We know these things and are assured of these things through the pages of Scripture. They are the Words of life, in which we find the Promise that gives us hope and the promises that sustain our hope. With such a hope in our hearts, we cannot help but rejoice!

## Journaling Suggestions

Give yourself some time to ponder over the things you have learned in this week's lesson. Journaling is a great way to get yourself thinking. Something about putting your thoughts into words helps you to make connections, draw conclusions. Light bulbs go on, and you understand something you didn't really know before. Here are some questions to get you started.

*1.* **Have you ever found yourself trying to improve your "resume" for God? What kinds of things do you do in order to impress Him?**

_____

_____

_____

_____

_____

_____

_____

_____

_____

_____

*2.* **What would life be like as a wandering sheep? What courage and comfort would you draw from having a Good Shepherd to lead you along the way?**

_____

_____

_____

_____

_____

_____

_____

_____

_____

*3.* **What does it mean when we say that Jesus is enough, or that hope is enough?**

_____

_____

_____

_____

_____

_____

_____

_____

_____

_____

_____

*4.* **You have been bought—redeemed—at a great price on Jesus' part. In what ways do we show our gratitude for His sacrifice?**

_____

_____

_____

_____

_____

_____

_____

_____

_____

*5.* **What makes the Bible so precious and so vital for every believer—what does it reveal, what does it provide?**

### JOURNALING QUOTE

*Journaling is not just about writing. It is also about listening. As you have your journal open, write as fast as your hand will go, and listen. When you are pouring your heart out or putting down your thoughts about a psalm, keep the ears of your spirit open to the voice of God. God speaks to me more when I have my journal out and my heart open than any other time in the day.*

Nicole Johnson

# Lesson 2

# Rejoicing in Hope

*"Rejoicing in hope, patient in tribulation, continuing steadfastly in prayer"*

Romans 12:12 NKJV

## Introduction by Luci Swindoll

When my brother Chuck was young, he loved sports. Many an evening mother called him to dinner from playing baseball, basketball, or football.

In his early teens Chuck begged for his own basketball. You can imagine his delight when Christmas morning came and there was a big gift-wrapped box with his name on it, exactly the size of his dreams. He was beside himself.

Ripping into the package, I'll never forget Chuck's disappointment when he pulled out the gift—a world globe. Although he wanted to show gratitude, regret was written all over his face. It was all Chuck could do to keep from crying and I didn't blame him. What was he going to do with the world? It wouldn't even bounce.

As I reflect on that long-ago Christmas I can't help but believe that gift was a metaphor of things to come. Listening to Chuck preach or reading his books tells me again and again that God had a great deal more in mind for my gifted brother than playing sand-lot basketball. His ministry today reaches across oceans and continents. His words have been translated into dozens of languages and Chuck's communication of God's truth has had a profound effect worldwide.

Today nothing means more to Chuck than taking the message of Christ all over the globe. Interestingly, my parents always wanted Chuck to be in ministry although they never mentioned it during our childhood. Maybe when they wrapped that Christmas gift they prayed a simple prayer asking God to use their son as a missionary. Whatever their intentions, that gift was a symbol of their hopes.

On Christmas morning, Chuck may not have gotten what he planned on, but he got his first glimpse of what God had planned for him—to take the Good News of Jesus Christ around the world. When I read the Bible verse that says, "Before I was born, the Lord called me to serve him", I can't help but think of Chuck.

We have hope! That's wonderful! Good to know. Lesson learned. So . . . now what?

It's really a joy to explore the pages of our Bibles and discover all the wonderful truths that have been placed there, but sometimes we are at a loss for what to do with those truths. We already know that we have hope. We know why we needed it, and we know how it was provided. We even know some of the characteristics of that hope. We have broken down "hope" into nice, tidy lists and definitions. But wait! These are not dry facts, to be listed in a notebook or filed on a hard drive. This week, we are going to turn to our Bibles again in order to stir up our hearts to rejoice in this hope. In order to do that, we'll take a look at how hope changes our lives. Just what does a hope-filled life look like? What does a hopeful person do from day to day? Some hopes are deferred until Christ's return, but which hopes are realized now, in our everyday lives?

The hope we have makes all the difference in the world. It fills us with joy. It dispels doubt and fear. It gives our hearts a place to rest. Hope is a reason for rejoicing!

## A PEEK AT OUR WEEK

- **Day One:** My Hope Is in the Lord
- **Day Two:** All the Difference in the World
- **Day Three:** A Reason for Rejoicing
- **Day Four:** My Joy and My Hope
- **Day Five:** Rest in Hope

## DAY ONE

# MY HOPE IS IN THE LORD

*"Happy are those who have the God of Israel as their helper, whose hope is in the LORD their God."*

Psalm 146:5 NLT

Don't you just love stories that put people on a great quest? There are so many stories of people going off on a quest. They seek honor, glory, freedom, redemption, answers, salvation, or even just treasure. Some set upon impossible tasks. Along the way they brave many dangers. They climb mountains, search caves, explore lost cities, translate strange carvings. They endure hardships, solve riddles, avoid traps, make friends, and vanquish foes. To go on a quest is to have an adventure. Some stories involve brave knights, others unlikely heroes. In ancient times, the stories included mythical champions like Jason, Odysseus, Hercules,

Perseus, and Sinbad. Then there were the knights, like Sir Lancelot, Sir Galahad, and Sir Gawain, who rescued fair maidens, slew dreaded dragons, and searched for the Holy Grail. Today we have Indiana Jones, who managed to find both the ark of the covenant *and* the Holy Grail. Frodo Baggins went on a quest to destroy the One Ring and save Middle Earth. One of Lara Croft's quests netted her Pandora's Box. In Christian literature, *Pilgrim's Progress* details a quest to the Celestial City, and C. S. Lewis' Prince Caspian sets off on the *Dawn Treader* to discover the fate of some missing noblemen. There have even been real-life examples of quests. Ponce de Leon, who is said to have discovered Florida, was on a quest to discover the Fountain of Youth. And Pizarro was the Spanish conquistador who sought the fabled El Dorado, the City of Gold, where the Incas lived.

What would it be like if God made each of us go on a quest in order to earn the hope for eternal life? What if the Scriptures said, "You must seek the tail feathers of a dodo bird, the horn of an aurochs, the right upper incisor of a wooly mammoth, and a scale from Leviathan in order to prove you are worthy of heaven." No wonder they're all extinct! But thankfully, we are not told to earn our right to hope. Our hope does not rest in our own strengths, abilities, bravery, cleverness, or luck. Aren't you glad? What a relief! Our hope rests solidly in the Lord, and that is a matter for rejoicing!

*1. The Bible is very clear. "When people work, their wages are not a gift. Workers earn what they receive" (Rom. 4:4 NLT). It's easy to fall into thinking that by being "good," we can earn God's approval. Paul tried to buy his hope in this way. But what did he come to realize, according to Galatians 2:19?*

Poor Paul. He was like the football player who scoops up a fumbled pass and runs with all his might in the wrong direction, scoring a goal for the opposing team. Paul, who was Saul in the beginning, was filled with earnest enthusiasm. He was a stickler for detail and followed the Law of Moses down to its finest points. He was admired, respected, envied, even feared. But the whole while, he was fighting against Christ. On this side of Damascus, though, Paul looked back at his life of strict obedience and achievement and just shook his head over the futility of it all. He'd gained a crystal clear understanding of God's gift of grace.

*2. There is no Do-It-Yourself handbook for salvation. Self-sufficiency and independent thinking won't get you very far with God. Before we can ever have hope, we must be humble enough to come to God, admitting that we need it. Take a look at the attitude described in these Scriptures.*

- What does Zephaniah 2:3 say that we should seek?

- What does God require of us, according to Micah 6:8?

- What does Peter say that we should do, according to 1 Peter 5:6?

- According to Psalm 149:4, what will God do for the humble?

*For the LORD takes pleasure in His people; He will beautify the humble with salvation.*

Psalm 149:4 NKJV

We have all tried it at some time—worked to meet some qualification, earn some right, or meet some standard that will make us worthy of God's love. But God wants to break through and show us that everything we need is ours for the asking. We cannot manufacture hope. We don't need to. Our hope is in the Lord.

*3. Here is a familiar passage from Paul's epistle to the church in Ephesus. Let's pick it apart a little bit.*

*For by grace you have been saved through faith, and that not of yourselves; it is the gift of God, not of works, lest anyone should boast.* —Ephesians 2:8, 9 NKJV

Salvation comes by _____. That means that God is the source of salvation.

We are saved through _____. That means believing.

Not of _____. No amount of gumption, determination, or elbow grease!

It is the _____ of _____. Every good gift and every perfect present comes from God (James 1:17).

Not of _____. Paul says it again, in another way, just to be clear.

Lest anyone should _____. Good-bye, bragging rights. Enter, humility!

If there is one fact we must fix in our minds today, it is that our hope rests in God and God alone. We can't beg, borrow, or plead our way into God's good graces. We can't find any back doors or loopholes in God's policies. No amount of creativity, sweetness, good intentions, or effort will sway God's decisions. Neither should we harbor other hopes in our heart. There's no contingency plan, no backup, no last resort. There is one way and only one way to be saved. God is our one and only source of hope.

*4. We have hope because Jesus saved us. He rescued us from a fate worse than death. There are numerous passages throughout the Scriptures that tell us about salvation. Each highlights a different facet of God's great gift. Here are just a few for you to match up.*

| | |
|---|---|
| ___ Luke 7:50 | a. "We were saved in this hope." |
| ___ Acts 2:21 | b. "There is no other name. . .by which we must be saved." |
| ___ Acts 4:12 | c. "According to His mercy He saved us." |
| ___ Romans 5:10 | d. "We shall be saved by His life." |
| ___ Romans 8:24 | e. "Your faith has saved you." |
| ___ Romans 10:9 | f. "[God] has saved us. . .according to His own purpose and grace." |
| ___ 2 Timothy 1:9 | g. "Whoever calls on the name of the Lord shall be saved." |
| ___ Titus 3:5 | h. "If you confess with your mouth . . . and believe in your heart. . .you will be saved." |

If you had to pin all your hopes on one thing, what would it be? Not a decision to be made lightly, is it? There are so many things that let us down. The one we pin our hopes on might turn out to be the very pin that bursts our bubble! People make mistakes. Things disappoint us. Expectations are left unmet. Even our friends can fail us. The stock market fluctuates. Laws have loopholes. Governments change with every election. Crops fail. Earthquakes, floods, and droughts destroy. Diseases infect. Accidents happen. Stuff breaks. Everything changes. Well, almost everything. In the midst of all the uncertainties of life, there is One who remains forever the same. Pin your hopes on Him!

*5.* **How can we be sure our hope is secure? It all depends on the One with whom it rests. What does Paul call God in 1 Corinthians 1:9? And what does David say about God's Word in Psalm 19:7?**

_____

_____

_____

_____

_____

_____

_____

_____

_____

When we look at how hope changes our lives in a day-to-day way, we can start with the verse that opened this lesson. "Happy are those who have the God of Israel as their helper, whose hope is in the LORD their God" (Ps. 146:5 NLT). This is what the hopeful person looks like—happy. But wait! If you look at the original language of the psalm, the writer is not talking about a feeling of happiness. Women who have put their trust in the Lord are not expected to be a continual fount of happy cheerfulness. The Hebrew word here could also be translated "blessed." Even when we don't feel happy, from God's perspective we are still blessed, and nothing can snatch His blessing away from us.

*6.* **Our lives are bound to God. He is the source of our hope, our joy, our peace, and the strength we need each day. He means everything to us, literally. The writers of Scripture tried to describe the Lord's role in their lives, each in unique ways. Look up these few Scriptures and finish the phrase found in each, beginning with "He is the . . ."**

| | |
|---|---|
| Deuteronomy 31:6 | He is the _____ |
| Deuteronomy 32:4 | He is the _____ |
| Psalm 24:10 | He is the _____ |
| Psalm 28:8 | He is the _____ |
| Ephesians 5:23 | He is the _____ |
| Colossians 1:15 | He is the _____ |
| Colossians 1:18 | He is the _____ |
| Hebrews 9:15 | He is the _____ |

The Lord is all of these things and more. Our hope is in Him. We could find it in no other. Our hope is secure because it rests in One who is faithful. We can depend upon Him because His promises are sure. Our hope in God makes us happy and blessed. In the life of a believer, hope makes all the difference in the world.

## PRAYING GOD'S PROMISES

Today's Scripture prayer is based on one of David's psalms of thanksgiving—Psalm 34:3–10. This is another passage that calls us happy: "Happy is the person who trusts Him" (Ps. 34:8 NCV).

*Savior God, I exalt Your name. I want everyone to join me in raising praises to You. Why am I so grateful? Because when I looked for You, You were there. When I called to You, You answered. You delivered me from my fears. When I give You all my attention, I am transformed—radiant. Though I am nothing, You came to my rescue. You saved me from my troubles. Your angels guard me. You are so good to me! I am happy that I placed my trust in You. I trust You. I respect You. I am in awe of Your majesty. You are kind to me, and have supplied me with everything I need. For me, You are enough. Amen.*

**Now you take a turn.** Take these few verses from Romans, which extol the simplicity of God's plan for salvation, and make them your own prayer. Explore with the Lord what it means to embrace Jesus, "body and soul." And take encouragement from the last phrase, which tells you that you'll never regret placing your trust in Jesus.

*Say the welcoming word to God—"Jesus is my Master"—embracing, body and soul, God's work of doing in us what He did in raising Jesus from the dead. That's it. You're not "doing" anything; you're simply calling out to God, trusting Him to do it for you. That's salvation. With your whole being you embrace God, setting things right, and then you say it, right out loud: "God has set everything right between Him and me!" Scripture reassures us, "No one who trusts God like this—heart and soul—will ever regret it."*

Romans 10:9–11 MSG

## DAY TWO

# ALL THE DIFFERENCE IN THE WORLD

*"You will again see the difference between good and evil people, between those who serve God and those who don't."*
Malachi 3:18 NCV

I love shopping. It's a sightseeing tour, a recreational sport, a fact-finding mission, a stress-reliever, a research project, a pick-me-up, and a party all wrapped into one. For most women, shopping is just plain fun. What's not to love? The whole process of going shopping gives us pleasure. We get to gussy up a bit, wear comfortable shoes, and spend hours meandering through aisles of stuff. Sometimes, we bring a friend along. Then, we can browse together through the shops, getting in a good visit while we see what's new this season. Every so often we'll interrupt ourselves by picking up something that catches our eye. "Look over there!" and "Isn't this cute?" "Oh! Wouldn't this be perfect for my sister!" We'll try on clothes, hats, and shoes. We'll redecorate our bathrooms, choose new drapes, and ooh and ahh over china patterns. Then, we'll leave the mall without actually buying anything. On the way back, we stop in somewhere for cappuccino and a cookie, then go home feeling refreshed.

Of course, there's a world of difference between shopping with our girlfriends and shopping with our husbands. (I hear those groans!) For the most part, men do not enjoy shopping in the same way women do. Bring them into the mall, and their eyes glaze over, their feet drag, and their faces go blank with the sheer mind-numbing pointlessness of browsing. They don't enjoy the process at all. But give a man a purpose, and it makes all the difference in the world. If I tell my husband, "I'm not sure what I'm looking for, but I'll know it when I find it," I can see the impatience mounting in his face. But if I tell him, "I need a white sweater, no buttons, three-quarter sleeves, with a scoop neckline," his eyes brighten with anticipation. He's a man on a mission. It's the thrill of the hunt. He's going to conquer that sweater.

Every day we're surrounded by people who are convinced of life's hopelessness. They feel trapped, restless, useless, and unhappy. They're numbed by the pointlessness of their lives. We are living in the very same world—breathing the same air, traveling the same highways, seeing the same sunsets. But our experience could not be more different. Hope makes all the difference in the world. Suddenly, we have a purpose. We have an end goal. We have something to look forward to. And, we can enjoy ourselves along the way.

*1. Hopeless people in this world are a lot like men at the mall— bewildered, disgruntled, or resigned to their fate. How does Scripture characterize these lost people?*

- How does Asaph describe hopeless people in Psalm 82:5?

- What does Jeremiah 50:6 compare a wandering people with?

- Even those who seem to have it all together are destined for what, according to Luke 9:25?

The imagery is consistent throughout Scripture. People who don't know God are lost. They are like sheep that have wandered away from the fold. They are like men and women stumbling around in the dark. They are following a road that leads to destruction. But Jesus offers hope, and hope changes everything. Hope is handing a map to the man lost on the side streets of a strange city. Hope is pointing out the North Star to the sailor navigating uncharted seas. Hope is whispering the secret of the maze into the ear of the woman who had given up any hope of making it to the end.

*2.* **Jesus knew all about our hopelessness. Look at how perfectly His goals matched up with our condition!**

- Who did Jesus come to save, according to Matthew 18:11?

_____

_____

- What did Jesus bring to those who were wandering in darkness, according to John 8:12?

_____

_____

When freshmen start college, they are all lumped together. Everybody starts by taking the basics—the "101" classes on the schedule. But as each semester passes, students are faced with a big choice. "What's your major?" With that decision made, the scholars are herded off in different directions. Sure, there are still choices to be made—"Do you have a minor?" "What's your specialty?"—but the general direction is now determined by their selected major. In a similar way, our decision to believe God and accept Jesus' gift of salvation has determined our course. Our choice has put us onto the narrow road that leads to Him. It is the decision that affects all subsequent ones.

*3.* **Several things shift when we become hope-filled people. One of those shifts happens in our perspective. Look at this picturesque translation of Paul's words in Colossians 3:2. Describe each perspective in terms of "before" and "after" Christ.**

*Don't shuffle along, eyes to the ground, absorbed with the things right in front of you. Look up, and be alert to what is going on around Christ—that's where the action is. See things from his perspective. —Colossians 3:2 MSG*

| BEFORE | AFTER |
|--------|-------|
| _____ | _____ |
| _____ | _____ |
| _____ | _____ |
| _____ | _____ |
| _____ | _____ |

*4. Not only does our perspective shift, our attitudes begin to undergo some adjustments. Look at the miraculous changes described in these Scripture passages:*

- Whose attitude should we mirror, according to Philippians 2:5?

- What does God think about this changed attitude in us, according to Romans 14:18?

- What support does God give to us in this attitude adjustment, according to Romans 15:5?

Hope remakes us into new women. It changes our state of mind. Our perspective changes, so that our eyes become fixed on the Lord. We try to put ourselves in His place—look at things in the same way that Jesus would have. Hope also works on our attitudes. Our heart tells us to put posing and pouting aside, trading grouchy "attitudes" for the attitude of Christ. When this happens, God is pleased with us. When we consider

> *If you serve Christ with this attitude, you will please God. And other people will approve of you, too.*
>
> Romans 14:18 NLT

the sheer magnitude of these changes in naturally selfish creatures, we begin to grasp the truly miraculous effect of hope on our heart.

*5. Hope works in our hearts here and now. But hope also gives us something to look forward to. Throughout his ministry, Paul spoke of his motivation. Along weary roads, amidst persecution, despite imprisonment, in the face of debates, shipwrecks, stonings, and more, Paul spoke of the goal that hope set before his eyes.*

- What keeps Paul going, according to Philippians 3:12–14?

_____

_____

- To what does Paul compare his life in 1 Corinthians 9:24?

_____

_____

- What is the quality of Paul's ultimate reward, according to 1 Corinthians 9:25?

_____

_____

> *I would have lost heart, unless I had believed that I would see the goodness of the LORD in the land of the living.*
>
> Psalm 27:13 NKJV

Paul's words are a cheer, a plea, a pep talk. He's saying, "Yes, it's hard sometimes. Sure, you'll have to apply yourself in order to reach your goal. But it'll be worth it. Trust me. It'll be worth everything you gave for it. In the end, you'll be glad you pressed on!"

*6. The hope we have makes all the difference in the world because it opens our eyes to new things, and it gives us something to look forward to. But it also gives us something to hold on to right now. What keeps David's hopes up, according to Psalm 27:13?*

_____

_____

_____

We used to be lost. We used to wander. We used to be in the dark. But that all changed. Now we have an incredible, amazing, irrepressible hope. Hope opens our eyes. Hope affects our attitudes. Hope gives us purpose. Hope sets a goal before us. Hope fills our lives with good things—the very goodness of God. Is it any wonder that we join Paul in saying that hope is our reason for rejoicing?

## PRAYING GOD'S PROMISES

Today's prayer is filled with thanks to God for rescuing us from darkness and sin and giving us His goodness. It is based on Psalm 107:10–16.

*Father of Lights, Thank You for pulling me out of the darkness. You have set me free, but I haven't forgotten what I was. I was a slave to sin once—bound by its chains and sentenced to death. There was rebellion in my heart. I ignored Your Word. I despised wisdom. On my own, I stumbled and fell. I thought I was alone. I didn't think anyone could help me. But in my desperation, I finally called out Your name. "Lord, save me!" And You did! You brought me out of darkness. You drove away all my distress, guilt, and shame. The chains of sin that bound me were broken forever, and I am no longer its slave. You have changed me. You have given me something to rejoice about. You have given me hope. I want everyone to hear about Your goodness. What You have done is wonderful, and I will never stop thanking You for it. Amen.*

Hope gives us a new perspective and helps us to see things from the Lord's point of view. Because of this, your Scripture prayer for today will be based on three verses from the Psalms. Each of these verses from *The Message* celebrates the understanding we gain when hope opens our eyes anew.

*Open your mouth and taste, open your eyes and see—how good God is. Blessed are you who run to him.*

Psalm 34:8 MSG

*Keep your eyes open for God, watch for his works; be alert for signs of his presence.*

Psalm 105:4 MSG

*Open my eyes so I can see what you show me of your miracle-wonders.*

Psalm 119:18 MSG

## DAY THREE

# A REASON FOR REJOICING

*"Be joyful because you have hope."*
Romans 12:12 NCV

Our family has an "any excuse for a party" policy. Why limit yourself to national holidays, birthdays, and anniversaries? When you're determined to have fun, it doesn't take much of a reason to get started. There are any number of grounds for a bit of merrymaking—the first crocuses of spring, pets' birthdays, a full moon, a rainy afternoon, hitting green lights at every intersection on the way home from work. Of course it's not always big doings. Our festivities might call for a dominos tournament, bubble baths all around, homemade buttermilk pancakes, or a trip to the library to check out all of the Dr. Seuss books.

Similarly, our salvation gives us a reason to rejoice. Paul urges us to rejoice in our hope (Rom. 5:2 NKJV). What, you may ask, is there to rejoice about? Well, let's see. God is so good to us, there must be a reason or two! We are loved unconditionally. We have been chosen. We have been granted mercy. We receive good gifts. We are given encouragement. We find hidden stores of patience. We enjoy the kindness of our sisters in the faith. We have peace that passes understanding. We are never alone. We know abundance. We witness God's miraculous working in our lives. We have been awed by God's majesty. God's Word is trustworthy. God provides for our every need. God's Spirit abides in us. God is always faithful. God keeps His promises. Prayers have been answered. Faith has been strengthened. Yes. I would definitely say that there are reasons to rejoice.

*1.* **What does a hopeful person look like? A hopeful person has discovered many reasons for rejoicing. Let's look at a few of the things we can be grateful for, starting with these three verses:**

- What is David's plea in Psalm 51:2?

- Paul gives us a "before and after" verse—Colossians 2:13. What did God do to bring about the change?

- What does God ask of us, according to 1 John 1:9?

Every day, even every hour, some little sin will crop up in our lives. A bit of tasty gossip, a sharp word, a sly motive, a covetous thought, an angry explosion—each needs to be confessed. And when we bring these failings before our Lord, He remains true to His promises and forgives us each sin. We are a forgiven people—cleansed from all unrighteousness. That is a reason for rejoicing.

*2. What does a hopeful person look like? A hopeful person lives with purpose, knowing the direction in which she should go. How does Isaiah describe the Lord's leading in Isaiah 30:21?*

> *Your ears shall hear a word behind you, saying, "This is the way, walk in it," Whenever you turn to the right hand or whenever you turn to the left.*
>
> Isaiah 30:21 NKJV

Have you been confronted yet with those new-fangled navigation systems they're putting into cars now? You key your starting point and your destination into this little box, and it keeps you from getting lost during your trip. You're toodling along the freeway, when suddenly the box chimes in. *"Ding, ding. Your exit is coming up in two miles."* Or *"Ding, ding. Left turn in point two miles."* When you do the right thing, the box approves by giving you another cheerful *"ding, ding."* If you happen to make a wrong turn, the box corrects you. *"Bong. Please return to the designated route."* Don't you wish God's directions for us were just as clear? As servants of God, we long to know what God's will for us might be. We want to do the right thing. We want to make the right decisions. We want to choose the right path. And God promises to lead us along, nudging us in the right direction, if we will just keep our hearts tuned to His promptings.

*3.* **God does not set us under way without first equipping us for the journey. These verses remind us that the Lord gives us His strength when we need it.**

___ Psalm 27:14    a. "The Lord will give strength to His people."

___ Psalm 29:11    b. "He gives power to the weak."

___ Psalm 119:28   c. "Wait on the Lord, and He will strengthen your heart."

___ Isaiah 35:3     d. "May God perfect, establish, strengthen, and settle you."

___ Isaiah 40:29    e. "Strengthen me according to Your word."

___ 1 Peter 5:10    f. "Strengthen weak hands and feeble knees."

When it comes to everyday existence, the thing we ask for most of all is the gumption to make it through another day. We just need someone to be on hand, to lend us a hand, or to hold our hand. Hopeful people know that their source of strength is close at hand. "Fear not, for I am with you; Be not dismayed, for I am your God. I will strengthen you, Yes, I will help you, I will uphold you with My righteous right hand" (Is. 41:10 NKJV). This, too, is a reason for rejoicing.

## Did You Know?

*In ancient times, the right hand held special significance. It was the hand of power, the hand that conferred blessings, the hand that supplied comfort. To sit at someone's right hand indicated victory and honor. To strengthen someone's right hand was to give them aid. And to hold someone's right hand was to lead them along the way. God offers to take us by the hand and guide us along: "For I, the* Lord *your God, will hold your right hand, saying to you, 'Fear not, I will help you' "* (Is. 41:13 NKJV).

*4. What does a hopeful person look like? A hopeful person lives with confidence that God is by her side and hears her every prayer. Finish the phrases found in these verses by filling in the blanks.*

These verses talk about prayer from our perspective:

_____  _____, O Lord, and _____my _____; _____me, for I _____ your _____. —Psalm 86:1 NLT

I_____ my _____ to the Lord; I _____ to Him, and He _____ my _____. —Psalm 120:1 NLT

These verses tell us what God says to us:

_____ to Me, and I will _____ you, and _____ you _____ and _____ things, which you do not know. —Jeremiah 33:3 NKJV

He shall _____upon Me, and I will _____ him; I will be _____ _____in trouble. I will _____him and _____him. —Psalm 91:15 NKJV

I, the Lord, am the one who _____your _____ and _____ over you. —Hosea 14:8 NCV

Jesus encouraged His followers to pray: "Until now you have asked nothing in My name. Ask, and you will receive, that your joy may be full" (John 16:24 NKJV). We know that God has heard our prayers. We see His hand working in our lives. We watch as circumstances come together in miraculous ways. We rejoice over every "Yes." We struggle to be patient for every "Wait." And we reaffirm our trust in Him whenever we face a "No." Prayer not only allows us to bare our hearts to our God, it allows

Him to answer us in very personal ways. This encourages us, and gives us yet another reason for rejoicing.

*5. The hopeful person is living a rich spiritual life, filled with countless reasons for rejoicing. Our lists could be endless, but here are just a few more.*

- Jeremiah 31:3

- Matthew 28:20

- Luke 12:22

- John 14:26

- John 14:27

- John 15:15

- 1 Thessalonians 4:13, 14

- 2 Peter 1:4

God touches a woman's heart in personal ways, letting her know that He is near, He is listening, and He loves her. I find this most often in the little details of life, which tie together in unexpected ways. It's going to the grocery store and finding out that everything on my list is on sale this week. It's getting a flash of inspiration, acting on it, and having everything turn out just right. It's realizing that the text for the pastor's sermon this week was in my devotions yesterday morning. It's little things that no one else would notice or know about, but they carry special significance for me. They are just like finding little love notes tucked away where I will find them. They affirm my hope and give me great joy.

### PRAYING GOD'S PROMISES

God has given us so many good things. For this we are thankful. He has given us so many reasons to rejoice. The three Scripture passages on which today's prayer is based all talk about the amazing benefits that we enjoy because we belong to God (Ps. 68:19; 103:2; 116:12).

*Benevolent Father, look what You have done! You have saved me. You are the God of my salvation. My soul rejoices. My soul blesses You for it. But You didn't stop there. Generous God, You have given me so much. Your gifts are many. You load me down with them. You heap them on my head. Every day I find something new to be grateful for. I never want to forget any of Your benefits. Oh, Lord, what can I do to repay You for the blessings? My heart belongs to You. Amen.*

**It is your turn.** Today, you will journal a prayer based on Paul's words in Ephesians 1:16–20. It's one of the apostle's own prayers, and in it he mentions the hope and all the riches that are ours through Jesus.

*I always remember you in my prayers, asking the God of our Lord Jesus Christ, the glorious Father, to give you a spirit of wisdom and revelation so that you will know him better. I pray also that you will have greater understanding in your heart so you will know the hope to which he has called us and that you will know how rich and glorious are the blessings God has promised his holy people. And you will know that God's power is very great for us who believe. That power is the same as the great strength God used to raise Christ from the dead and put him at his right side in the heavenly world.*

Ephesians 1:16–20 NCV

## DAY FOUR

# MY JOY AND MY HOPE

*"Oh! May the God of green hope fill you up with joy,*
*fill you up with peace, so that your believing lives, filled with the*
*life-giving energy of the Holy Spirit, will brim over with hope!"*

Romans 15:13 MSG

Do you remember learning elementary grammar, and having nouns explained to you? At first, we were told that a noun was a person, place, or thing. Cat, dog, mother, father, church, school, Dick, Jane, Iowa, and Ohio—they're all nouns. But later, the teacher tagged on another bit to the definition. Now a noun was a person, place, thing, *or idea*. We needed a loophole in our definition for all the intangibles of life—"Truth, justice, and the American way," freedom, peace, pride, trust, love, hope, and yes, joy. These ideas were all something we understood, because many of them were emotions we had experienced—fear, jealousy, confusion, pity, sadness, happiness. Lumping them together into a category was no problem, but defining them wasn't always so easy.

So how do we define joy? The dictionary defines joy as "intense and especially ecstatic or exultant happiness." That's not too bad, but as believers, we're more concerned with the biblical definition. You see, joy cannot be defined as intense happiness, because joy and happiness are two very different things. Joy is a feeling. But oddly enough, biblical joy isn't something we produce within ourselves. Joy comes as a gift—a spiritual gift. God gives it to us.

*1. What does joy look like? Scripture gives us many, many examples. Look at a handful of verses here, each describing the overflowing of joy.*

- What arrangements for joyful worship did David make in 1 Chronicles 15:16?

- How is the sound of rejoicing described during Solomon's coronation in 1 Kings 1:40?

- When the Jews had rebuilt the fallen temple, what was the atmosphere surrounding its dedication, according to Nehemiah 12:43?

Great joy. Resounding joy. The people's joy was so great, and their cheering so loud, that it would have drowned out the roar of the crowds at a football stadium. Isn't that the way it is at your house? No? All right, how about Luke's description of the response of a joyful person— "Rejoice in that day and leap for joy!" (Luke 6:23 NKJV). No? Still not you? Well, how about this verse, which could describe a more personal joy.

"You shall see and become radiant, and your heart shall swell with joy" (Is. 60:5 NKJV). Loudly or softly, actively or with quiet bliss, a believer's life will be characterized by joy.

*2. The Bible speaks of joy and rejoicing over and over again. They tell us who rejoices, what a joyful attitude looks like, how joy is shown, why we have joy, and where our joy comes from. These verses give us just a sampling. Match them with their text.*

___ Deuteronomy 28:47    a. Those who sow in tears will reap in joy.

___ Psalm 5:11    b. We receive joy when fellow believers refresh our hearts.

___ Psalm 51:12    c. Serve the Lord with joy and gladness of heart.

___ Psalm 126:5    d. Everlasting joy shall be ours.

___ Isaiah 12:3    e. Jesus' joy remains with us so that our joy may be full.

___ Isaiah 51:11    f. Let those who love Your name be joyful in You.

___ Isaiah 55:12    g. You shall go out with joy.

___ Isaiah 65:14    h. Restore me to the joy of my salvation.

___ John 15:11    i. Pray with joy.

___ Philippians 1:4    j. We will draw water from the wells of salvation with joy.

___ Philemon 1:20    k. My servants shall sing for joy of heart.

What a list! It's kind of impressive to catalog so many facts about joy. But don't forget—never forget—that joy cannot be summed up in a tidy list. Joy is not quite that reasonable or refined, and certainly not that dry. Joy is not a nod of approval or a polite smile. Joy cannot be expressed in calm statements. Joy demands exclamation points! Joy is somersaults and handsprings! Joy is cartwheels through a field of daisies! Joy is tumultuous, vibrant, and giddy. Joy is a fruit of the Spirit—a sure sign of the Holy Spirit's presence in our heart. Joy can exist in combination with the strangest of emotions—like fear (Matt. 28:8) and suffering (1 Pet. 1:6)—without losing its potency. Joy is so unique, and so often defies logic or description, that God's prophet Habakkuk even resorted to using the term "joy" to explain itself. He turned joy into a verb—"I will joy in the God of my salvation."

*3.* **Who is able to know the joy of the Lord? Obviously, those of us with hope-filled lives experience joy. Who else is mentioned in the Scriptures as joyful?**

- People with what two characteristics are mentioned in Psalm 32:11 as having joy?

- What kind of person receives joy from the Lord, according to Ecclesiastes 2:26?

- Who does Isaiah 29:19 say shall increase their joy?

Look at the descriptions of joyful people—good, righteous, upright, humble. What's more, remember that joy is a fruit of the Spirit. Do you understand the ramifications of this? Check it out. Who is missing from this list of joyful people? Non-Christians. Unbelievers. Hopeless people. Can someone without hope understand joy? No! Joy is not only a gift, it is a privilege reserved for God's own children!

4. *What does Nehemiah say that the joy of the Lord is to His people?*

_____

_____

_____

_____

_____

_____

_____

_____

_____

Joy comes only from God, so the joy of the Lord is a God-given happiness. This joy is our "strength," according to Nehemiah. Since joy is God-given, the strength we draw from it comes from the Lord as well. The Hebrew word for strength means "refuge" or "place of safety." The people's refuge was God. In Nehemiah's time, the Jews had built a wall to guard their temple and their city. But their true refuge, their real strength was in the Lord. Though intangible, the joy harbored in their hearts served to remind them that their lives were safe in God's mighty hand.

5. *Just as our hope is real because of the One upon whom it is fixed, so our joy is real and lasting because of its Source. Look at each of these verses, and write down the source of joy mentioned in each one.*

Psalm 43:4—"There I will go to the altar of God, to God—the source of all my joy. I will praise you with my harp, O God, my God!" (NLT).

_____

_____

Jeremiah 15:16—"Your words are what sustain me. They bring me great joy and are my heart's delight" (NLT).

John 17:13—"These things I speak in the world, that they may have My joy fulfilled in themselves" (NKJV).

Acts 13:52—"And the disciples were filled with joy and with the Holy Spirit" (NKJV).

1 John 1:4—"These things we write to you that your joy may be full" (NKJV).

3 John 1:4—"I have no greater joy than to hear that my children walk in truth" (NKJV).

What brings joy into our lives? God the Father does. Jesus does. The Holy Spirit comes with joy. God's Word is an inexhaustible source of joy. Just as we need to know where to turn in order to find hope, we must know where to look for joy.

6. *As wonderful as this joy we know is now, Scripture tells us that it is only a foretaste—a glimpse of the full joy we will know in heaven. Here are two such verses from God's Word.*

- Where does David say he will find fullness of joy, according to Psalm 16:11?

- What does Jesus say we can enter if we are faithful servants of the Father, according to Matthew 25:21?

*In Your presence is fullness of joy; at Your right hand are pleasures forevermore.*

Psalm 16:11 NKJV

Remember the verse that opened up today's lesson? "Oh! May the God of green hope fill you up with joy, fill you up with peace, so that your believing lives, filled with the life-giving energy of the Holy Spirit, will brim over with hope!" God gives us joy, that feeling of happy assurance in our spirits, as a gift. It reminds us that we are in His hands. It fills us with peace. And it makes our hearts to brim over with hope—a hope we can rest in.

## PRAYING GOD'S PROMISES

We know joy because we have hope. They go hand in hand. We cling to hope in the face of our struggles, and in the same way, we must hang on to joy. This day's Scripture prayer is based on one of Jesus' illustrations in John 16:21, 22, which reminds us that all of our sorrows will fade away completely when we see Jesus someday.

*God of Joy, teach me to be patient in this world. I have so many responsibilities—so much work to do. I am often sad. Things spin out of my control. My heart has seen and known such raw pain. You say that I will have joy in spite of it. That is what I am asking You for today. That is what I will hold on to today. You say that this life is like a woman in labor. I remember that feeling—dread, anticipation, helplessness, fear, pain, determination, and, yes, hope. And at that moment when that hope was realized, all the other feelings faded away. The anguish was worth the joy of holding a new son or daughter. You promise us that life's struggles will be worth it.*

*You have not seen Christ, but still you love him. You cannot see him now, but you believe in him. So you are filled with a joy that cannot be explained, a joy full of glory.*

1 Peter 1:8 NCV

*Now may the God of hope fill you with all joy and peace in believing, that you may abound in hope by the power of the Holy Spirit.*

Romans 15:13 NKJV

*Now to Him who is able to keep you from stumbling, And to present you faultless Before the presence of His glory with exceeding joy, To God our Savior, Who alone is wise, Be glory and majesty, Dominion and power, Both now and forever. Amen.*

Jude 24–25 NKJV

*Someday, our hope will be realized. Someday, we will see You, and our hearts will rejoice. The joy we hold then will last forever. Lord, give me the determination to hold on to hope until, with joy, I see Your face. Amen.*

Take a little time to journal a prayer of your own here. Each of the verses in the margin here talks about the joy we have here, today, and the joy we wait for with anticipation at Christ's return. Make them your own words now.

---

## DAY FIVE

# REST IN HOPE

*"My heart is glad, and my glory rejoices; my flesh also will rest in hope."*
Psalm 16:9 NKJV

Especially after a time of spiritual refreshment, we begin to feel as if we could take on the world! Woo hoo! It doesn't matter what might come our way. Bring it on! We can take it. Things are well in hand. We've got it covered. No problem. No worries. Like Bob the Builder, we cheerfully say, "Can we fix it? Yes, we can!" We're like an outfielder as the ball sails in our direction. We run forward, yelling, "I've got it! I've got it!" We wave God off and make the play ourselves. We try to be the hero. We've got Little Red Hen Syndrome, and walk around saying, "I'll do it myself!" We go it alone for a while, working out of our own strength. Forgetting the Source of our strength and joy, we start making it up as we go along. But it doesn't take long for us to falter. Pretty soon, we find ourselves burned out. The joy fades out of our work. We realize we're only going through the motions.

God knows us so well. He sees that independent streak, that stubborn nature, that proud resistance to accept help or charity. He isn't fooled by our bravado. He's just waiting for us to break down and admit our deep need. What a relief it is to rest. One of the reasons we can rejoice is that we are not our own source of hope. We do not have to save ourselves. We don't need to plan our own escape. God gives us hope, and we can rest in it.

*1. Now and again, we catch ourselves putting our trust in something other than God. Scripture gives us plenty of examples of what not to lean on in this life. Match up several of them here.*

| | | |
|---|---|---|
| ___ Psalm 20:7 | a. carved images and false idols |
| ___ Psalm 44:6 | b. oppression and robbery |
| ___ Psalm 49:6 | c. empty words |
| ___ Psalm 62:10 | d. horses and chariots |
| ___ Psalm 118:8, 9 | e. wealth and riches |
| ___ Isaiah 42:17 | f. ourselves |
| ___ Isaiah 59:4 | g. bows and swords |
| ___ Jeremiah 7:8 | h. lying words |
| ___ Mark 10:24 | i. men and princes |
| ___ 2 Corinthians 1:9 | j. riches |

Solomon was truly wise when he said, "Trust in the LORD with all your heart, and lean not on your own understanding" (Prov. 3:5 NKJV). We know the difference between right and wrong, but so many things lure our attention away from the path in front of us. The world makes so many convincing promises, but it is asking us to put our trust in passing things. Wishful thinking, easy money, rising stardom, a quick fix, instant gratification, secret thrills, little indulgences. It's no wonder that God so often refers to us as children. Sin skews our judgment and prompts us to make childish blunders. We're like kids, who are told to eat our broccoli because it's good for us. Given the chance, we'd trade it all for sugary grape bubble gum. As believers, we need to shut our ears to the siren song of worldly pleasures. We must cling to the motto: "Father Knows Best." We need to trust God completely and follow His lead.

*2. Is God strong enough to lean upon? Is God worthy of the trust we place in Him? Take a look at Psalm 9:10. Why does David say we can trust in the Lord?*

> *Those who know Your name will put their trust in You; for You, Lord, have not forsaken those who seek You.*
>
> Psalm 9:10 NKJV

Think about it—if you know God, really know Him, then you'll trust Him. He's no con artist, trying to pull a fast one on us. He's not some used car salesman, trying to sell us a lemon. He's not making campaign promises that will never be kept. God is God, and the reputation attached to His name is matchless. He doesn't just have good character. He invented good character! He doesn't just show us goodness and love. He *is* goodness and He *is* love. To know God is to trust Him implicitly.

*3. Let's look through a few more verses in order to explore our trust in the Lord.*

- How long has the psalmist trusted in God, according to Psalm 71:5?

- How would God's ways and God's words be characterized, according to 2 Samuel 22:31?

- In 1 Timothy 4:10, what was Paul willing to endure because he trusted God?

- With what does David entrust the Lord, according to Psalm 25:20?

Look at these testimonials. David trusted God so much that he placed his very soul into the Lord's keeping. He trusted God with all that he had and all that he was—right down to the hidden person of his heart. And look at Paul. He trusted God enough to endure hardships in this life. Paul acknowledged that his path was difficult, but he was willing to walk that hard road because he trusted it was where God had placed him. What about us? David's pledge seems easy to match. It's pretty easy to trust God with our souls for eternity. But what about Paul's level of trust? Are we willing to trust God, even when it is hard to do? We should give God all of our lives, and trust Him to lead us rightly—not just do as we please and give Him the leftovers.

*4. There's a big difference between saying that you trust God and living as if you do. We can fool the whole world, but who knows the difference, according to Nahum 1:7?*

We've got all kinds of sayings that we pass on to our kids. Things that have nothing to do with the Lord or faith—but we can adapt them! For instance, "You can't fool mother nature." Or how about the stories we tell about dear old Santa Claus. "He's making a list and checking it twice. Gonna find out who's naughty and nice." Well, you can't fool your Heavenly Father. He may not keep a checklist, but He knows who's been naughty and who's being nice. God knows exactly what's in our hearts, no matter how convincingly we might behave in public. He knows whether we're just putting on a pretense of trust or if we have placed ourselves solidly into His hands.

*5. Our trust in God is always rewarded. We already know that we have hope in Him. We already know that we are blessed. We have learned that we have joy from the Lord. Let's add a few more to the list from these verses from the Psalms about trust.*

- Why do people trust themselves to God, according to Psalm 36:7?

- What is God able to do for those who place their trust in Him, according to Psalm 37:5?

● In what does the psalmist trust, according to Psalm 52:8?

_____

_____

● And in Psalm 56:3, what does trust dispel?

_____

_____

*6. Hope is a reason for rejoicing, in and of itself. A life that rests in hope has placed its trust in the Lord. Look at Psalm 143:8 NKJV together with me, because it sums up our lesson so well.*

*Cause me to hear Your lovingkindness in the morning,*
    *For in You do I trust;*
*Cause me to know the way in which I should walk,*
    *For I lift up my soul to You.*

● What character quality of God is mentioned in this verse, which the psalmist trusts?

_____

_____

● Who does he trust?

_____

_____

● Because of this trust, what is he willing to do?

_____

_____

● What does he trust God with, placing it in His care?

_____

_____

We must trust the God of Hope. We need to learn to lean on Him, to follow Him, to live for Him. We place our lives in His hands. We rest in the hope of His promises. Resting in hope—another key to rejoicing in hope.

### PRAYING GOD'S PROMISES

God is worthy of our trust, and when our hopes are placed in Him, we can rest assured that they will come to pass. Today's Scripture prayer is based on Job 11:13–20 and the unwanted words of advice found there. Though this so-called friend of Job isn't helping matters any, he does give a beautiful description of the process of confession, forgiveness, and trust.

_Trustworthy Lord, I am reaching out to You. Help me to prepare my heart to be in Your presence. Forgive me, and I will be able to lift my spotless face up to You. Put aside my iniquities. Drive out the wickedness in my heart. Place me on a firm foundation—make me steadfast. Push aside all the doubts that plague me—help me to trust You. Wash away all my misery. Then, my life will shine with righteousness. It will be as if the night has passed and the dawn has come. I will be brighter than the noonday. Then, I will be secure. I will have hope. I will rest in safety. I will be fearless. Everyone will be able to see the difference You have made in my life. Lord, I am reaching out to You. Make me new. Amen._

In the New King James Version, David prays to "the God of my strength, in whom I will trust" (2 Sam. 22:3). Don't you love how David's prayers come out sounding like poetry? Today, let's take a look at this same prayer of David as it is translated in _The Message_. It can inspire the prayer you journal today.

*God is bedrock under my feet, the castle in which I live, my rescuing knight. My God—the high crag where I run for dear life, hiding behind the boulders, safe in the granite hideout; My mountaintop refuge, he saves me from ruthless men. I sing to God the Praise-Lofty, and find myself safe and saved.*

2 Samuel 22:2–4 MSG

## Conclusion

This week we have considered the fact that hope is a reason for great rejoicing in every believer's heart. "The hope of the righteous will be gladness" (Prov. 10:28 NKJV). All people live in the same world and witness the beauty of God's creation, but the experience for those with hope and those who still wander in darkness is vastly different. Hope makes all the difference in the world. Since our hope is in the Lord, we don't have to depend on our own strengths, abilities, bravery, cleverness, or luck to gain it. It is a part of God's gift of salvation. Hopeful people are joyful people, for the Lord has placed joy in their hearts. "You have put gladness in my heart" (Ps. 4:7 NKJV). So, what does the hopeful life look like? Hopeful people are recognized by many of the good things God has given to them—forgiveness, purpose, strength, peace, answered prayer, and joy. "Light and gladness, joy and honor" (Esth. 8:16 NKJV). And hopeful people have put their trust in God, for both the path they walk now and for eternal life that is to come.

This hope in which we rejoice has changed our lives. Now we have purpose. We know peace. We know joy. The gifts that accompany hope serve to strengthen our trust in God. And as our faith and trust in God are made strong, so in turn is our hope made unshakeable!

## JOURNALING SUGGESTIONS

*1.* During Day One, we looked at all the things that God can be for His people. He is our King, our Refuge, our Mediator. Who is God for you? What roles does He take in your spiritual life?

*2.* How has hope changed your perspectives, your attitudes, or your goals?

*3.* **Paul talks about his hope in Christ as one of the greatest motivators for his ministry. What usually motivates you? What kinds of things are you now finding that hope can motivate you to do?**

_____

_____

_____

_____

_____

_____

_____

_____

*4.* **How would you put joy into words?**

_____

_____

_____

_____

_____

_____

_____

_____

*5.* **What kinds of things are hard for you to trust completely into God's hands?**

_____

_____

### JOURNALING QUOTE

*Encountering my journal keeps me awake to God and to myself. A journal is a tool, a flower, a canvas, a safety deposit box, a cup of coffee with a friend. It can hold your dreams, record your life, challenge your thinking, refresh your soul, tickle your sides, and redirect your steps.*

Nicole Johnson

# LESSON 3

# UNWAVERING HOPE

*"This hope we have as an anchor of the soul, both sure and steadfast"*

Hebrews 6:19 NKJV

## INTRODUCTION BY THELMA WELLS

One of the common phrases I've heard all my life is, "Don't get your hopes up." That's always intrigued me because I've wondered, *"If you don't get them up, where else are they going?"* But my great-grandmother, Granny who raised me, would always counteract that phrase by saying, "Keep your hopes up." That made more sense to me. During my life, however, there have been a few times when I seemed to have no hope. I thought my prayers were not being answered. People I longed for were not available. Dreams I dreamt seemingly were not coming true. Some of my bubbles about life burst when I experienced Real Life 101. The word *hope* began to intrigue me with its different applications.

Sometimes *hope* is a metaphor for a childish wish.

Vanessa, my eight-year-old granddaughter, put her order in to me (Grammy) for some white tennis shoes with fat shoestrings. She hoped that Grammy would get the right ones the first time. When I did, her hopes were fulfilled with something tangible.

Sometimes *hope* is a serious desire for a blessing or a miracle.

Bryna, my four-year-old granddaughter, had surgery on her stomach. The family hoped she would go through the surgery and heal without complications. She did and we were thankful.

Sometimes *hope* is a quest for accomplishing goals and positions. Lesa, my daughter, has dreams of expanding her business.

Sometimes *hope* is a daydream for some kind of fantasy. I'm hoping to be able to sit on the couch in a big dress, drink peach tea, and read a good book or watch a movie without having to think about a deadline.

These suggestions of hope may seem trivial. But none of these is the real hope of life. There is a hope that is only found in Jesus Christ. Hebrews 10:23 advises us to, "Let us hold fast the confession of our hope without wavering, for He who promised is faithful." The marvelous fact about our hope in Christ is that He never does anything for us that is not good to us.

When God gives us hope, He gives us many other good gifts as well. Last week we talked about just a few of them—lovingkindness, peace, mercy, forgiveness, answered prayer, and joy. All of these blessings strengthen our trust in the Lord. And as our trust is deepened, our hope is held more firmly. This week, we're going to look at unwavering hope. Though we hope in something that cannot be seen, our faith in God is unshakeable. Each of us must cling tightly to what we know is true, but Scripture reminds us that we are not alone. All Christians share the same hope, and we are united by it. For the sake of hope, believers have been willing to endure hardships and suffering. We will look at what we are willing to do for the sake of hope. And finally, we'll look at how hope anchors us in our spiritual life, linking us steadfastly to the Lord.

### A Peek at Our Week:

- **Day One:** Unseen
- **Day Two:** One Hope
- **Day Three:** Unshakeable
- **Day Four:** For Hope's Sake
- **Day Five:** Hope Is an Anchor

## DAY ONE

## UNSEEN

*"Where then is my hope? As for my hope, who can see it?"*

Job 17:15 NKJV

Remember the song from *The Sound of Music* that the nuns sing about Maria? "How do you solve a problem like Maria?" Compared to the serene and serious nuns of the abbey, Maria's just so flighty and out of control. Despairing over ever making Maria understand how to be a proper novice, the nuns break into song (don't we all), and compare dealing with her to other impossible things. "How do you take a cloud and pin it down?" "How do you keep a wave upon the sand?" "How do you hold a moonbeam in your hand?" As believers, we are faced with the equally unlikely task of holding tightly to something we cannot touch or see. From the world's perspective, that's just plain crazy. We live in a society that wants concrete evidence—driver's license, photo ID, birth certificates, social security numbers, passports, fingerprints, DNA samples. Since God seems reluctant to come up with the goods, the world writes Him off. But as unlikely as our task seems, believers are doing it every day. Oh, we're not pinning clouds down, but we're grabbing on to hope. Our trust in the unseen is unshakeable. Our faith in the invisible God remains steadfastly at the center of our lives. And as outrageous as that might seem, our lives prove hope's validity. An unswervingly hope-filled life silences the scoffers.

*1. Paul offers us a pretty logical explanation for why our hope is unseen. What reason does he offer in Romans 8:24, 25?*

Just because we cannot pin God down or hold hope in our hands doesn't mean that they don't exist. We know that we're not making this up as we go along. We're not supposed to see our hopes realized right now. Hope wouldn't be hope if it had arrived already. That's why Christianity is so often called a "faith." It's like Hebrews 11:1 says, "Faith is the substance of things hoped for, the evidence of things not seen" (NKJV). Our life of faith is characterized by hope, and the faithful life serves as proof that our hope is real and true.

*2. In every believer's life there come days when we wish we had something more solid to latch on to. Wouldn't it be nice to have our faith confirmed by something we could see or hold in our hands? But what does Paul remind us in 2 Corinthians 5:7?*

Remember what Jesus said to Thomas—I'll-believe-it-when-I-see-it Thomas? "Thomas, because you have seen Me, you have believed. Blessed are those who have not seen and yet have believed" (John 20:29 NKJV). When it comes to hope and faith, we must simply trust that our Heavenly Father knows what He's doing. It doesn't pay to pout because our hope is unseen. There are times when parents have to resort to saying, "Because I said so," to their children. And this is the way God deals with us. We live as believers—trusting in a God, in a hope that we cannot see—because God says to.

*3. Our hope is invisible. Our faith rests in the unseen. It's no surprise, really, considering what the Scriptures tell us about the God in whom our faith and hope rest.*

- What is Paul's description of God in the benediction found in 1 Timothy 1:17?

- Moses is remembered for his faith. He lived as if. . .what, according to Hebrews 11:27?

● Though God is invisible, what can we see clearly, according to Romans 1:20?

_____

_____

Whenever we try to explain the spiritual world, the thing that we most often compare it to is the wind. Wind can be gentle, whispering across our skin. Wind makes garden flowers nod. Wind rustles through the branches of the trees. Wind makes the sheets snap on the clothesline. Wind sculpts sand dunes, whips up ocean waves, and drives vast ships across the sea. The wind's force can also have devastating effects—tornadoes, whirlwinds, hurricanes, sand storms. All of these effects cannot be denied, and yet the wind is invisible. Unseen, but undeniable.

*4. Solomon wanted to build a temple to God. What reason did he give for its construction in 1 Kings 8:13?*

_____

_____

_____

_____

_____

_____

_____

_____

_____

_____

_____

_____

_____

_____

## Did You Know?

*David dreamed of building a temple for God, but his Lord told him no. So David turned his attention to making preparations. For years he accumulated the building supplies that would be needed for construction. He stockpiled cedar from Lebanon. He bought up all the gold in the region. When his son, Solomon, finally finished the glorious temple in Jerusalem, it was made possible in part by the groundwork laid by his father.*

When God designed a place on this earth to meet with His people, He gave very specific instructions. The plans for the tabernacle were specific, right down to the tent pegs. When Solomon built a temple for God at Jerusalem, he made it the most magnificent building in the world. It was a visible sign of God's presence among His people. The temple became a place of prayer, of sacrifice, of worship, and of teaching. This was their meeting place, where they could rendezvous with the invisible God.

*5. **Though we often feel as if God made the entire universe just for our benefit, we are blind to some of its intricacies. Scripture confirms that though creation points us to its Creator, much of what God made is invisible to our eyes.***

| | |
|---|---|
| ___ John 3:5 | a. God created everything, both visible and invisible things. |
| ___ Romans 8:9 | b. The invisible Jerusalem is filled with innumerable angels. |
| ___ Ephesians 6:12 | c. God is invisible, but clearly present in our lives. |
| ___ Colossians 1:16 | d. Our real life is hidden—invisible to others. |
| ___ Colossians 3:3 | e. We battle against the powers of an unseen world. |

___ Hebrews 11:10      f. The invisible moves the visible, much like the wind.

___ Hebrews 12:22      g. Abraham fixed his eyes on an unseen but eternal city.

*6. How does Paul describe Jesus in Colossians 1:15?*

_____

_____

_____

_____

_____

_____

_____

*But if God Himself has taken up residence in your life, you can hardly be thinking more of yourself than of Him. Anyone, of course, who has not welcomed this invisible but clearly present God, the Spirit of Christ, won't know what we're talking about.*

Romans 8:9 MSG

The unseen world collided with the world we know so well when Jesus arrived among us. He was "God with us," but Jesus was no invisible man. We could not see the Father, but behold—we could see the Son! God became a man—touchable, hearable, seeable, knowable. Jesus told His followers, "He who has seen Me has seen the Father" (John 14:9 NKJV). And Jesus came with a message of hope. True, this hope is yet unseen, but it is the one hope that all believers share.

## PRAYING GOD'S PROMISES

Our hope is unseen, but it is a certainty. It is a cause for joy. It strengthens our faith. We long to see our hope fulfilled, but we rest in the assurance of our hope. God will bring it to pass. Today's prayer is based on a Scripture that speaks of our waiting—Romans 8:19–25.

*You realize, don't you, that you are the temple of God, and God Himself is present in you? No one will get by with vandalizing God's temple, you can be sure of that. God's temple is sacred—and you, remember, are the temple. Don't fool yourself. Don't think that you can be wise merely by being up-to-date with the times. Be God's fool—that's the path to true wisdom. What the world calls smart, God calls stupid. It's written in Scripture, He exposes the chicanery of the chic. The Master sees through the smoke screens of the know-it-alls. I don't want to hear any of you bragging about yourself or anyone else. Everything is already yours as a gift—Paul, Apollos, Peter, the world, life, death, the present, the future—all of it is yours, and you are privileged to be in union with Christ, who is in union with God.*

1 Corinthians 3:16–23 MSG

*God of Glory, I am waiting for You. All the earth has been placed under the curse. It groans under the weight. All creation is waiting breathlessly for its release. It pants like a woman in labor. My own heart longs for the curse's lifting. Then I will know glorious freedom. Death and decay will be abolished. We will be released from all pain and suffering. I cannot help but look forward to the day when all these hopes will be realized. I hang on to this hope. I am waiting patiently. I am waiting confidently. Amen.*

***Now it is your turn.*** Take a look at 1 Corinthians 3:16–23, which is printed for you in the margin. Solomon built a visible temple in which the Jews could meet with God. Paul tells us that *we* are God's temple now, because we are privileged to be united with Christ and have the Holy Spirit dwelling within. Read through this passage and make it your prayer today.

# DAY TWO

# ONE HOPE

*"There is one body and one Spirit,
just as you were called in one hope of your calling."*

Ephesians 4:4 NKJV

Variety. The thesaurus equates variety with words like "assortment," "miscellany," and "diversity." Most folks like a little variety—it makes things more interesting. We shop in variety stores, buy things in variety packs, and watch variety shows on television. We like to be presented with a variety of flavors at the ice cream parlor. We want to find a wide variety of toppings at the salad bar. We thrill at the variety of papers supplied by scrapbooking stores. We have vegetable medleys, combination pizzas, and boxes of assorted chocolates. One of my favorite sayings is, "Variety is the spice of life." Variety is a good thing.

When God created, He showed off His great capacity for variety. He made hills and valleys, trees and grasses, clouds and stones. He made a wide variety of creatures. Birds come in a variety of colors. Fish come in a variety of shapes. Mammals come in a variety of sizes. And this amazing diversity continues, right on down to the details. Consider the snowflakes—no two are alike. Consider our fingerprints—each person's is unique. God made each of us individually. Each one is a reflection of God's creative genius. There are no copies, no duplicates, no replicas. We are each a one-of-a-kind masterpiece.

Within the church, believers come in an amazing variety as well. Men and women, young and old. We are all uniquely gifted. We each have our part to play in the body of Christ. We come from all over the world—every people, every nation, every language. And yet, we all have one thing in common. We all share one hope.

*1. It's nice to know that we are God's workmanship (Eph. 2:10). It's encouraging to know that we are special. Yet individuality is not pleasant if it only leads to jealousy, bickering, and divisions. What does David say is a very good thing in Psalm 133:1?*

## Did You Know?

*Good workmanship was esteemed in Bible times. In the days of King Josiah, the men who made repairs to the Temple were so trusted that no foreman was needed to oversee their handiwork (2 Kin. 22:7). Their integrity was assumed, and their craftsmanship was of the highest quality. The Greek word translated "workmanship" in Ephesians 2:10 means that we are each a result of God's careful handiwork, His masterpieces.*

Why is it so hard for people to just get along? From the time we were little, Sesame Street characters and Mr. Rogers have tried to teach us the value of cooperation. But our natural bent is to put ourselves first and to fight for our own way in every situation. David sings the praises of unity—how good and how pleasant it is! Imagine how much nicer life would be if we achieved harmony with one another. Peaceful homes, peaceful work environments, peaceful congregations. Wouldn't it be nice to spend a pleasant hour at the dinner table, to experience a pleasant car ride, to sit in on a pleasant committee meeting?

*2. Jesus didn't set the standard for us without first blazing the trail. He knew all about our uniqueness and differences, but He longed for us to live in unity—bonded together by our shared hope in Him.*

- What was Jesus' prayer for His followers, found in John 17:11?

- According to John 17:22, whose relationship are we mirroring when we live in unity?

- What will result from the unity of believers, according to John 17:21?

Jesus' prayer was that we would all be one. One hope. One Spirit. One Lord. One faith. One Church. Unity of mind. Unity of purpose. Solidarity. Collaboration. Like-mindedness. Alliance. Helpfulness. Harmony. Partnership. Unanimity. Joint effort. Teamwork. Cooperation. Do these words make up an accurate description of your relationship with other believers?

*3.* **What did Paul tell the Colossian church was the most important thing to do, according to Colossians 3:14? What was his reasoning?**

> *Do all these things; but most important, love each other. Love is what holds you all together in perfect unity.*
>
> Colossians 3:14 NCV

Our love for one another was to become the hallmark of Christianity. It was to be our *modus operandi*, our calling card, our trademark, our distinguishing characteristic, our seal of authenticity. Jesus said, "By this all will know that you are My disciples, if you have love for one another" (John 13:35 NKJV). Paul said that it is our love that holds us together in perfect unity.

*4. There are many believers, and we all share one hope. What do these verses tell us about our oneness in Christ?*

- According to John 10:16, what did Jesus say about the Jews and the Gentiles?

  _____

  _____

- What divisions were set aside by Christ, according to Paul in Galatians 3:28?

  _____

  _____

We are all one in the eyes of God. He does see our uniqueness and our differences. After all, He thought them up. But with God there is no partiality. The prince is no greater than the pauper. "But many that are first shall be last; and the last shall be first" (Matt. 19:30 KJV). We are on a level playing field. No one has an advantage over any other. No one gets an edge, a head start, an inside track. We are all measured against the same standard—Christ. We can't influence the judge. We can't locate a loophole. We can't sweet-talk our way in. . .or out. There can be no exemptions, no shortcuts, no exceptions. We all have access to God through prayer. We all know His promises and His blessings. We all have known His mercy and grace, His forgiveness and His love. And when we're in His flock, we all share the very same hope.

*5. Throughout the New Testament, those who share one hope are urged to be of one mind.*

- What was Paul's plea to the Corinthian church, recorded in 1 Corinthians 1:10?

  _____

  _____

● How does Peter describe unity in 1 Peter 3:8?

_____

_____

This whole "be of one mind" thing seems like a pretty tall order. Just look at all the different personality types there are, and all the differences of opinion. I'm not even sure I *want* to think the same way as some people I know! But when Paul tells us to be of one mind, he's not saying that we all have to think the same way. He's saying that we need to think the *same thing* toward one another. We need to be in agreement. The key here is not having uniformity of thought, but having common attitudes and purpose. Paul wants us to live in harmony with fellow believers.

6. *Take a look at these other Scripture passages. Each gives us one small facet of what unity in Christ should look like. Match the verse with its summary statement.*

___ Acts 4:24          a. Be of good comfort, be of one mind, live in peace.

___ Acts 4:32          b. Unity of faith comes with maturity.

___ 2 Corinthians 13:11   c. We should be united in our efforts to spread the gospel.

___ Ephesians 4:3       d. Believers should be united in hearts and spirit.

___ Ephesians 4:13      e. Believers should be united in prayer.

___ Philippians 1:27     f. We are united by the Holy Spirit.

Anne of Green Gables is such a sweet character in literature. No one could deny that she was just a little different than anyone else in Avonlea. Her unique outlook on life made many people look askance at that redheaded snippet of an orphan girl. But Anne-spelled-with-an-E stayed true to her own heart, and along the way, met many kindred spirits. Did you know that we—we Women of Faith—have kindred spirits? Think for a minute of the countless souls who are our sisters in Christ. We are united, and have become kindred spirits because we have something in common. God's love, grace, joy, peace, promises, blessings—and hope.

## PRAYING GOD'S PROMISES

Paul's epistles are full of little pep talks. He urges and encourages, orders and exhorts his children in the faith to do the right thing. Today's Scripture prayer is based on Paul's words in Philippians 1:27–30, in which he mentions the need for a united stand and unity of purpose among believers.

*Matchless God, I want to live in a way that brings honor to the gospel, to Jesus, to You. Help me to stand strong in the Word. Teach me Your way. Show me Your promises. Strengthen my faith. Open my eyes to the kindred spirits all around me—my brothers and sisters in the faith. Help us to work together with one purpose. Spread Your Good News through our united efforts. Keep us focused on the task You have set for us. It is an honor just to know You. I feel privileged to count Jesus as my brother. Give me the spiritual fortitude to stand for Jesus even in the face of struggles. If I must suffer for His sake, may it bring You glory. Open my eyes to the struggles of my sisters in the faith, and use me to strengthen and support them. Help me to share with them the life-changing encouragement that hope brings. Amen.*

Take a little time now to read through this passage from one of Peter's epistles a few times. Consider how this apostle's exhortations would affect your relationship with other believers. Let his words sink in, then form them into your own prayer here.

*Finally, all of you be of one mind, having compassion for one another; love as brothers, be tenderhearted, be courteous; not returning evil for evil or reviling for reviling, but on the contrary blessing, knowing that you were called to this, that you may inherit a blessing. For "He who would love life and see good days, Let him refrain his tongue from evil, and his lips from speaking deceit. Let him turn away from evil and do good; let him seek peace and pursue it. For the eyes of the LORD are on the righteous, and His ears are open to their prayers; but the face of the LORD is against those who do evil."*

1 Peter 3:8–12 NKJV

# DAY THREE

# UNSHAKEABLE

*"He only is my rock and my salvation;*
*He is my defense; I shall not be moved."*

Psalm 62:6 NKJV

I don't have to go any further than my kitchen cupboards to find examples of unshakeable things. There's the lumpy baking soda that has to be pressed through a sieve in order to render it useable. There's the salt-encrusted shaker on the back of my stove—moisture seems to have solidified its contents. There's the solid mass of onion powder that I can't bear to throw out, so I chip it apart with a knife every time I need a little. Oh yes. There's the annual de-clumping of the Christmas cookie sprinkles. I don't know how the icing gets into those bottles every year—but it does. Unshakeable, immovable, steadfast—not good household terms, to my way of thinking. They bring to mind the window over my kitchen sink that cannot be budged—I haven't been able to open it for three years now! There are all manner of substances stuck on, ground in, and indelibly marked onto my furniture. Rings on my coffee table. Sharpie marker scrawled across the worktable in the garage. Spelling words carved into my dining room table. To put it more biblically, the lime buildup behind my bathroom faucet is not easily shaken. The orange soda stains on my cream-colored carpeting shall not be moved.

Though the thought of irremovable things around the house makes me cringe a little inside, there are some very good things that can never be moved. One of those things is our hope!

*[Abraham], contrary to hope, in hope believed, so that he became the father of many nations, according to what was spoken.*

Romans 4:18 NKJV

*1.* **The "Father of Faith" is Abraham. He believed God would keep His word, even when the promises He made seemed impossible. How does Paul describe Abraham's faith in Romans 4:18?**

Who doesn't love seeing the "little guy" beat the odds? The Bible is filled with unlikely people making good. A younger son's receiving the inheritance due to the firstborn (Jacob). A convict rising to prominent governmental office (Joseph). A meek and mumbling man leading an entire nation out of slavery (Moses). The youngest son, whose job it was to tend the sheep, selected by God as the future king of Israel (David). An orphaned commoner chosen to be the next queen of Persia (Esther). With such inspiring stories to support our faith, is it any wonder that we're always rooting for the underdog?

*2.* **How would your hope be characterized? Confident? Assured? Unshakeable? Take a look at these verses, which all remind us why we can stand firm.**

- In Psalm 112:6, what does the psalmist say that the righteous can never be?

- Why was David so confident that he couldn't be shaken, according to Acts 2:25?

- What was Timothy's mission, according to 1 Thessalonians 3:1–3?

## *Did You Know?*

*Paul's epistles were not sent to the various churches of the New Testament through their local post offices. They didn't even have a pony express. The most reliable way to send correspondence from one city to the next was via courier. This is one reason why Paul sent Timothy to the church in Thessalonica. He couldn't trust that all-important letter to any old courier, so it went in the pocket of a trusted friend.*

Sometimes we need to hang on to hope, even when life's little frustrations try to shake us up. We need tenacity—you know, stick-to-itive-ness. We need to be hard to shake. Like a dryer sheet that clings to the inside of your pant leg. Like a five-year-old niece who's determined to tag along. Like a tune that runs around and around in your head all day long. Like a trailing train of toilet paper, caught on the heel of your shoe. We need to stick like glue, like gum on a shoe. We need to grab hold and never let go. Remember what David said? He was able to stand firm because he kept the Lord before His face. That means he kept his eyes on God, focused on Him, followed Him, made Him the priority, gave Him his attention, pursued Him. With his eyes full of his Lord, no wonder David's faith and hope were unshakeable!

*3. Hold on tight! That message comes through loud and clear. But hold on to what? Take a look at these passages—each gives us a slightly different facet of what it is we are holding on to. You can match them up.*

___ Deuteronomy 11:22        a. Hold fast to the Word.

___ Job 2:9                         b. Hold fast to the Lord your God.

___ Job 27:6                        c. Hold fast to the pattern of living
                                              set out in Scripture.

___ 1 Corinthians 15:2         d. Hold fast to righteousness.

___ 1 Thessalonians 5:21      e. Hold fast to your integrity.

___ 2 Timothy 1:13             f. Hold fast to what is good.

We read about the lives of saints and martyrs. They held fast to their hope in the face of terrible suffering and persecution. For the sake of the Lord, they gave up a normal way of life, their homes, their families, their freedom, even their lives. Such stories are inspirational—stirring our hearts to stay true no matter what hardships we might face someday. We know we can rise to the challenge of a life-and-death struggle. We can strengthen our resolve in the face of a crisis. We are even willing to make the ultimate sacrifice. But have we ever considered the tenacity required to remain faithful in ordinary ways? We may never be called to die for our Lord, but we have been called to live for Him. In the face of inconveniences. At the cost of total obscurity. Through seasons of routine, even boring days. Sacrificing our personal preferences. Even when we don't see the point. Is your hope unshakeable, even when life is mundane?

*4. Some days, we have a clear view of our objectives. Other times, we just don't feel terribly hopeful. We are on shaky ground when we rely on our feelings. How do these verses tell us to hang on to hope?*

Lamentations 3:21—This I _____ to my _____, therefore I have _____.

Hebrews 10:23—Let us _____ _____ the _____ of our _____ without _____, for He who _____ is _____.

Revelation 3:3—_____ therefore how you have _____ and _____; _____ and _____.

Revelation 3:11—Behold! I am coming quickly! _____ _____ what you have, that no one may _____ your _____.

Notice how often we are urged to recall and remember? Those who are unshakeable in their hope are able to recall God's promises and remember their confession of faith. Feelings have their ups and downs, but we don't want our trust in God to follow that erratic path. Faith involves a choice—a decision, an act of the will, a determination. We can decide to hang in there with the Lord and remind ourselves of the commitment we've made. When we hold onto hope, no one can take it away from us.

*5. What does Hebrew 3:6 say that we are holding on to? How long should we hold on?*

_____

_____

_____

_____

_____

_____

_____

Just look at that! *"Hold fast the confidence and the rejoicing of the hope"* (Heb. 3:6 NKJV). It's another example of our hope in God being associated with confidence and with rejoicing. When we hope in the Lord, we aren't pining away after something that might never come to pass. We will see our hope someday. When Jesus says *"Hold fast what you have till I come"* (Rev. 2:25 NKJV), we can do so with confidence and tenacious joy.

*6.* **What does Hebrews 12:28 say we will receive, if we cling to hope? And what kind of life are we urged to live until we receive it?**

### PRAYING GOD'S PROMISES

While we are waiting for our hope to be revealed, Paul says we should be living in reverence and serving God. We can gather some insight into what that kind of life looks like from Paul's lists of little reminders in the epistles. He often closed a letter with last words of advice. Today's prayer is based on one of those lists, found in 1 Thessalonians 5:16–24.

*God of Peace, Teach me to accept Your gifts and make use of Your blessings. I don't want to see Your precious promises go to waste! You have offered me joy—let me always be joyful. You have offered* to lend me Your ear—let me pray continually. You have given me all I need—let me show proper gratitude. Make me wise, so that I will know the difference between good and evil. Train my heart to long for good. Give me the strength of mind to turn away from that which I know is evil. Make me pure. Make me worthy of Your name. I belong to You—spirit, soul, and body. I want to serve You. I trust You. Help me to hang on until Jesus comes. Amen.

***Now it's your turn.*** Here are a couple of verses from Joshua. As he neared the end of his life, he urged the children of God to stay true to the Lord. Make them your prayer as you journal here.

*Take careful heed to do the commandment and the law which Moses the servant of the LORD commanded you, to love the LORD your God, to walk in all His ways, to keep His commandments, to hold fast to Him, and to serve Him with all your heart and with all your soul.*

Joshua 22:5 NKJV

*Choose for yourselves this day whom you will serve . . .But as for me and my house, we will serve the LORD.*

Joshua 24:15 NKJV

## DAY FOUR

# FOR HOPE'S SAKE

*"For this hope's sake. . .I am accused."*

Acts 26:7 NKJV

We will go way out of our way to impress people—things that we wouldn't dream of doing on an everyday basis. And there's nothing like a visit from out-of-town guests to get us moving. We'll scrub the floors, wash the windows, shampoo the carpets, sweep the driveway. We'll clean out the coat closet, dust the chandelier, and bring out all the candles. Since it's a grand occasion, we'll plan a four-course meal, shop at the gourmet grocers, and color coordinate the condiments. We'll buy fresh flowers, iron the tablecloth, dust off the good china, and shine up the crystal stemware. We'll make points on all the toilet paper rolls, fill all the candy dishes with chocolate truffles, and buy fresh fruit for the bowl on the coffee table. We'll fill the salt and pepper shakers, locate the gravy boat, and press linen napkins. As the big day approaches, we take extra pains over little details—garnishes, place cards, potpourri, guest soaps, background music. Nothing is left undone. Everything is perfect.

So what does that all have to do with hope? Just this comparison. We are willing to put so much effort into making a good impression—work and plan and prepare for a guest's sake. Have you ever considered what are you would be willing to do for hope's sake?

*1. Every individual is called to something a little different in this life. We each have our place, our own responsibilities. But Paul beseeches us to remember that we are all called to one thing. What does Romans 12:1 say that is?*

We can no longer be called our own—we've been bought with a price (1 Cor. 6:20). So instead of living for our own pleasure, for our own fulfillment, for our own purposes, we are urged to live for God. Now that isn't easy to hear, and it's even less easy to accomplish. That's why we call it a sacrifice.

*2. Paul endured much for the sake of the gospel—shipwrecks, stonings, imprisonment, beatings. Yet this amazing man was able to rejoice in his suffering. These next couple verses help explain why.*

- Who do believers suffer for, according to Philippians 1:29?

- Who was Paul suffering for, according to Colossians 1:24?

- Who else was Paul enduring all things for, according to 2 Timothy 2:10?

Paul might have preferred to avoid some of the trials he encountered. Can you imagine what it must have been like to be adrift on the ocean after a shipwreck? Beaten with whips and rods? Locked away in dank, dark prison cells? The recipient of frequent death threats? Left for dead after having rocks hurled down upon you? Yet Paul willingly persevered. For the sake of Jesus, for the sake of fellow believers, for the sake of those who needed to hear the gospel. It was a small price to pay in exchange for the hope he held tightly, and for the hope he was able to carry to others.

*3.* *Jesus' prayer was, "Not my will, but thine, be done"* (Luke 22:42 KJV). *Followers of Christ have been asked to do much for His sake. Here is a sampling from the New Testament. Match them up with their verses.*

___ Matthew 5:10      a. leave your former life behind for His name's sake

___ Matthew 5:11      b. falsely accused of evil for Christ's sake

___ Matthew 10:18      c. counted as a fool for the sake of Christ

___ Matthew 10:39      d. persecuted for righteousness' sake

___ Matthew 19:29      e. charges brought against you for Christ's sake

___ Luke 6:22      f. hated, excluded, and a marred reputation for His sake

___ 1 Corinthians 4:10      g. lose your life for Christ's sake

___ 1 Peter 2:13      h. submit to government and laws for the Lord's sake

Jesus warned us that we could expect trials and persecution. The world that shunned Him and plotted against Him could hardly be expected to embrace one of His followers with open arms! Not many of us will face shipwrecks or stonings, but there are subtler forms of attack. Compromise, apathy, selective belief, ignorance, busyness, social acceptability, selfishness, and unrealistic expectations all chip away at a life lived for the Lord.

*4. What is Paul's list of things he'd be willing to endure for Jesus' sake, according to 2 Corinthians 12:10? And even more importantly, what reason does he give for this willingness?*

_____

_____

_____

_____

_____

_____

_____

_____

_____

_____

_____

_____

Paul wasn't facing these trails because he loved living on the edge. It wasn't for thrills that he put his life on the line. He didn't get a rush out of staying one step ahead of local authorities. He wasn't some kind of .007 super-spy out on Mission Impossible. Paul was just an average guy. He admitted that he was weak (2 Cor. 12:9). He was considered a fool (1 Cor. 1:27). He begged fellow believers to pray that he would be able to speak with boldness (Eph. 6:19). Paul knew that God has "chosen the foolish things of the world to put to shame the wise, and God has chosen the weak things of the world to put to shame the things which are mighty" (1 Cor. 1:27 NKJV). So Paul allowed God to display supernatural power in his life. He took God on His word when He said, "My grace is sufficient for you, for My strength is made perfect in weakness" (2 Cor. 12:9 NKJV). To this, Paul replied, "Once I heard that, I was glad to let it happen. I quit focusing on the handicap and began appreciating the gift. It was a case of Christ's strength moving in on my weakness" (2 Cor. 12:9 MSG).

*5. How does Paul sum up Christ's sacrifice and our response in 2 Corinthians 5:15?*

_____

_____

_____

_____

_____

_____

_____

_____

*6. What are we willing to do for hope's sake? What do we live for? What are the consequences of such a life? These verses all give us a little more insight into these questions. Match them up.*

___ Psalm 58:11     a. We are dead to sin and able to live for the glory of God.

___ Matthew 6:33     b. We have died to the law so that we might live for God.

___ Romans 2:7     c. Those who live for God will be rewarded.

___ Romans 2:8     d. We have died to sin so that we can live for righteousness.

___ Romans 6:11     e. By doing good, we live for God's glory.

___ 1 Corinthians 8:6     f. Those who live for themselves will experience God's wrath.

___ Galatians 2:19     g. Your day-to-day needs will be provided if you live for God.

___ 1 Peter 2:24     h. All things come from God, and we live for Him.

Today's lesson serves as a reminder and a challenge. We have hope—hurray! But we also have a responsibility to live for God. What are you willing to do for hope's sake?

## PRAYING GOD'S PROMISES

Today's prayer is based on one of the letters to the churches, found in Revelation 2:1–5. In it, the Lord praises the church at Ephesus for the ways in which they are living for Him, and He exhorts them to return to the love they once had for Him.

*Giver of Life, You have given me so much! I owe everything to You—my life, my hope, and strength for each and every day. I want to learn more about You—to know You better. Help me to listen attentively when I hear teaching on the Word. Give me discernment, to ferret out false statements and half truths. I want to live for You, to work hard and never give up. Grant me patience whenever I am called to suffer for Your name. I want to cling unshakably to hope, and never let go. But most of all, Lord, I want to love You. Change me so that I can love You aright. Draw my mind, my heart, and all my affections in Your direction. I want You to have all my heart, all my soul, all my mind, and all my strength. Amen.*

Take a look at the two Scripture passages in the margin. Both talk about learning to live for God. Make them your prayer as you journal here.

*The love of Christ controls us, because we know that One died for all, so all have died. Christ died for all so that those who live would not continue to live for themselves. He died for them and was raised from the dead so that they would live for him.*

2 Corinthians 5:14, 15 NCV

*It was the law that put me to death, and I died to the law so that I can now live for God. I was put to death on the cross with Christ, and I do not live anymore—it is Christ who lives in me. I still live in my body, but I live by faith in the Son of God who loved me and gave himself to save me.*

Galatians 2:19, 20 NCV

## DAY FIVE

# HOPE IS AN ANCHOR

*"This hope we have as an anchor of the soul, both sure and steadfast."*
Hebrews 6:19 NKJV

Hope is unseen. It is made out of the same whispery nothings as thoughts and dreams and wishes. It's as hard to pin down as faith. It is insubstantial. It is invisible. It is intangible. It is hidden from our eyes. So doesn't it seem strange to associate something so elusive with an anchor? According to the dictionary, an anchor is "an iron instrument which is attached to a ship by a cable (rope or chain), and which, being cast overboard, lays hold of the earth by a fluke or hook and thus retains the ship in a particular station" (Dictionary.com). Anchors are big, hooked, and heavy. We associate anchors with sailors and ships and seagulls and barnacles. They're bulky. They're rusty. They plummet into the water and sink like stones. But thankfully, when we're talking about hope as our anchor, we're not referring to a sinking feeling in the pit of our stomachs.

The writer of Hebrews isn't saying that hope is a literal anchor. He's drawing a comparison between what an anchor does for its ship and what hope does for our hearts. The anchor of a ship is its source of security and stability. Blustery winds, choppy waves, strong currents—they'll have no effect. We cannot be pulled off course. An anchor has come to stand for that on which we depend for safety.

*1. Hope is our anchor. Let's do a little comparison of translations on this verse, shall we? For each version, notice what hope is compared to (e.g., an anchor), what words describe it (e.g., "sure" and "steadfast"), and what it allows us to do (enter God's presence). You might like to use different colored pencils to highlight each of these.*

**New King James Version**—This hope we have as an anchor of the soul, both sure and steadfast, and which enters the Presence behind the veil.

**New Century Version**—We have this hope as an anchor for the soul, sure and strong. It enters behind the curtain in the Most Holy Place in heaven.

**New Living Translation**—This confidence is like a strong and trustworthy anchor for our souls. It leads us through the curtain of heaven into God's inner sanctuary.

**New International Version**—We have this hope as an anchor for the soul, firm and secure. It enters the inner sanctuary behind the curtain.

**Today's English Version**—We have this hope as an anchor for our lives. It is safe and sure, and goes through the curtain of the heavenly temple into the inner sanctuary.

**The Message**—It's an unbreakable spiritual lifeline, reaching past all appearances right to the very presence of God.

**Phillips**—This hope we hold as the utterly reliable anchor for our souls, fixed in the very certainty of God himself in Heaven.

Hope holds us steady. Hope ties our hearts to heaven. Hope keeps us from going adrift. Hope secures us, so that we can go about our business. When we are anchored, we do not run the risk of straying off course, capsizing in a storm, or being dashed against the rocks.

*2.* **When we don't have an anchor, we're liable to get tossed about quite a bit.**

- What is doubt compared to in James 1:6?

  _____

  _____

- What can happen to newbies in the faith, according to Ephesians 4:14?

  _____

  _____

When we let doubt take over our minds, James says we're tossed—literally like a cork bobbing wildly in the ocean's waves. Hope stabilizes our emotions, putting us on an even keel. Our souls know the full range of feeling—happiness, worry, sorrow, curiosity, pity, sincerity, fear. Yet in the midst of tumultuous emotions, hope holds us steady.

*3.* **What does Hebrews 10:23 urge us to do? Why?**

_____

_____

_____

_____

_____

_____

*4.* **What example does Abraham leave us of unwavering hope? Paul tells us in Romans 4:20, 21.**

_____

_____

Hold fast. Do not waver. The message is the same throughout Scripture. The reason behind it is the same as well. Hold on to your hope. Do not waver in your faith. For the Lord has made a promise, and He cannot lie. His words are always true. He will keep His word. We will see all our hope fulfilled.

*5.* *We don't want to doubt. We don't want to waver. What we long to be is steadfast. Steadfast before the Lord—anchored by the hope He gives.*

Psalm 51:10—_____in me a _____
_____, O God, and _____ a
_____ spirit within me.

Psalm 57:7—My _____ is _____, O
God, my _____ is _____.

1 Corinthians 15:58—Therefore, my beloved brethren, be
_____, _____,
always _____ in the work of the Lord.

1 Peter 5:9—Resist [the devil], _____ in the
_____.

Hebrews 3:14—We have become partakers of Christ if we
_____ the beginning of our _____
_____ to the end.

Hope is our anchor. It's not a ship's anchor, which plumbs the depths of the ocean and digs into the sandy bottom. It's an anchor

*For it was by God's own decision that the Son has in himself the full nature of God. Through the Son, then, God decided to bring the whole universe back to himself. God made peace through his Son's sacrificial death on the cross and so brought back to himself all things, both on earth and in heaven. At one time you were far away from God and were his enemies because of the evil things you did and thought. But now, by means of the physical death of his Son, God has made you his friends, in order to bring you, holy, pure, and faultless, into his presence. You must, of course, continue faithful on a firm and sure foundation, and must not allow yourselves to be shaken from the hope you gained when you heard the gospel. It is of this gospel that I, Paul, became a servant—this gospel which has been preached to everybody in the world.*

Colossians 1:19–23 TEV

that rests in the secret places of heaven. Our anchor is in our Lord's hand. He is the One holding our hope. No matter how difficult circumstances may get, we can trust, knowing that our hope is secure.

## PRAYING GOD'S PROMISES

The Lord is our hope, and hope is our anchor. We could not wish for a surer foundation. Today's prayer is based on a few verses from one of Paul's letters to Timothy (2 Tim. 2:19–21). He reminds the younger man of his solid footing and urges him to live honorably because of it.

*Anchor of My Soul, You have placed me on a firm footing. Everything around me seems to shift and change on a whim, but You stand. You know me—how amazing is that? You know me because I belong to You. That fills my heart with a sense of pride—I like being Yours. I want my life to honor the name of Jesus, so aid me as I flee from iniquities into Your strong arms. I may not be the most renowned of believers. I may not be a shining example of faith. No one would call me a vessel of gold, or even of silver. But even if I am carved from humble wood or shaped from humbler clay, I am Your handiwork. I am Yours. Cleanse me so that You can use me. Make me a vessel of honor. Prepare me to do good in Your name. Amen.*

Read through the passage from Colossians in the margin—read through it a couple of times. It contains one of the verses that exhorts us to continue in faithfulness because of our firm foundation in the Lord, but the whole paragraph is worthy of consideration. Personalize it as a prayer today.

## CONCLUSION

Our hope is an anchor—sure and steadying. Our hope is unshake-able, for it rests in the One who cannot be moved. We share this hope with fellow believers, and we are able to encourage one another in hope along the way. For hope's sake, we will live for the Lord—giving up our preferences for something far better. We trust the God of hope, whose many blessings meet our every need. Hope abounds in our hearts, and its abundance touches every area of life.

## JOURNALING SUGGESTIONS

*1.* *Would having something tangible—something you could touch and see—make your faith any stronger than it is now? Why, or why not?*

*2.* *What kinds of things do you tell bickering children to assure them that they are equally loved for their unique place in the family? Compare that to the "sibling rivalry" that crops up in the church. Do the same answers apply?*

*3.* *Jesus said that His followers would be known because of their love for one another. Love would be their trademark. What would you want to be known for? What would your trademark be?*

**4.** *If holding on to hope meant letting go of everything else, what would be hardest to release, even if you knew God would hold on to it for you?*

**5.** *Does the thought of being anchored make you feel secure, confident, or does it make you feel tied down, limited?*

### JOURNALING QUOTE

*It was on the pages of my journal that I learned to bring my heart to God. I prayed in my journal. I cried as I wrote. I wondered out loud why things had happened the way they had. I asked God questions. I offered requests to God and then highlighted them when He answered. Journaling became for me the tangible representation of my relationship with God and others, and my wrestlings with the world around me.*

Nicole Johnson

# LESSON 4
# ABOUNDING IN HOPE

*"Now may the God of hope fill you with all joy and peace in believing,
that you may abound in hope by the power of the Holy Spirit."*

Romans 15:13 NKJV

## INTRODUCTION BY SHEILA WALSH

It was a familiar question, and I smiled as my doctor asked it.

"Do you think that this year you might get into a regular work-out regime?"

"I hope so," I replied.

"Is that a no?" she continued.

I laughed. "I really want to but I'm so busy. Christian is in school, and we are traveling a lot and. . ."

"There will always be a lot to do, Sheila," she said. "This is something you need to do for yourself."

I knew she was right, but in my life there is a vast cavern between the things I am committed to doing and the things that I *hope* to get to. The things I hope to get to might as well have a nap, as it could be a long, lonely winter!

My flimsy reply exposed the discrepancy between true hope and wishful thinking.

When I consider the admonition of Paul to the church in Rome to be abounding in hope, it is clear that Paul is not referring to wishful thinking. He doesn't mean, "Let's cross our fingers and see if we can make it through one more year." He is speaking of the kind of hope that casts its light and grace over every area of our lives. To abound means to thrive and to flourish. So how do we do that?

We live in uncertain times. We don't know what each day will bring for us or for those we love. Every time we turn on the news or open a newspaper, there are fresh wars and rumors of wars. But here is what we do know; here is the truth that we can stake our life on.

We know that God is in control and He is good.

We know that He has a perfect plan for our life, and nothing can happen to us today or tomorrow that has not first passed through His merciful hands.

We know that whatever we face, we will not face it alone.

Christian hope is not a fragile thing. It is rock solid, and by God's grace we can abound!

Let's do a quick review. We would not have any hope at all if it had not been for God. Our hope is in Jesus, and it is a cause for rejoicing in our lives. We can rest in this hope, trusting God to bring it to pass. Our hope is steadfast, unwavering in the face of feelings or circumstances. This week our theme is abounding hope. You've heard the saying, "Hope springs eternal"? Well, it does! Hope spills over from our hearts into all areas of life. We do not rest in hope as one would rest on her laurels. By no means! In fact, the sureness of our hope serves to motivate, compel, and spur us on. Hope is our armor in the face of conflict. Hope makes something that God has called "good" into something that is altogether priceless. Hope mellows us and teaches us patience. And hope gives us a life that will continue in a never-ending tale of faith, hope, and love.

## A PEEK AT OUR WEEK

- **Day One:** Faith, Hope, and Love
- **Day Two:** The Patience of Hope
- **Day Three:** Hope Is Our Armor
- **Day Four:** Hope, and Our Crown of Rejoicing
- **Day Five:** A Life of Hope

## DAY ONE

# FAITH, HOPE, AND LOVE

*"And now abide faith, hope, love, these three;*
*but the greatest of these is love."*
1 Corinthians 13:13 NKJV

There is an old saying that things happen in threes—for good or for bad. I don't know about that, but there does seem to be a fascination with things that come in triplicate. There have certainly been a lot of famous trios that come to mind. How about the Three Musketeers—Arthos, Porthos, and Aramis. Tradition holds that there were Three Wise Men— Melchior, Balthasar, and Casper. There were the Andrews Sisters, drawn close around the old microphone, boogie-woogieing in tight harmony. There are the Three Tenors, whose shoulder-to-shoulder performances raise the rafters. Even the world of television seems to have decided that things come in threes. My Three Sons—Ernie, Robbie, and Chip. There were three Cartwright boys on Bonanza—Adam, Hoss, and Little Joe. When the Bradys got married, each brought a threesome of children. Three boys—Greg, Peter, and Bobby. Three girls—Marsha, Jan, and Cindy. There were always three roommates on Three's Company. There were always three young women playing Charlie's Angels. There were Three Stooges. Donald Duck had three nephews—Huey, Dewey, and Louie. Daisy Duck had a trio of nieces—April, May, and June. Trios even hit the big screen. Anyone remember the Three Amigos or Three Men and a Baby? And of course, there are some very important threes that come from Scripture. Namely, the Trinity—Father, Son, and Holy Spirit. There were the famous siblings from Bethany—Lazarus, Mary, and Martha. There was Jesus' inner circle, the three disciples closest to Him—Peter, James, and John. But today, we're going to look at another famous threesome—faith, hope, and love.

*1. Let's review our definitions before we move on. What does the Bible tell us that faith, hope, and love are?*

- Hebrews 11:1—Faith is



- Romans 8:24, 25—Hope is



- 1 Corinthians 13:4–7—Love is



Faith is believing, trusting. It is an assent of the mind to the truth God has revealed. And it is a submission to that truth in everyday life.

Hope is the confident expectation of something good. In the Old Testament, words like "refuge" and "shelter" take the place of hope—meaning hope is the thing that protects us when everything around us crumbles.

Love, contrary to popular thought, is not a feeling. Love is an attribute of God—He possessed it before He had someone to show it to. In the Old Testament, there are over forty Hebrew words to describe God's love—that's how complex it is, and difficult to define. In Christians, love is a virtue. It is the opposite of selfishness. Love happens when we put others first—it is complete selflessness.

*2. These three wonderful gifts from God seem to go hand in hand . . . in hand. And the Love Chapter in 1 Corinthians isn't the only place where they show up together. What does Paul say in 1 Thessalonians 1:3?*

"Remembering without ceasing your _____ of _____, _____ of _____, and _____ of _____ in our Lord Jesus Christ in the sight of our God and Father" (NKJV).

So why do we find these three attributes or qualities of the faith hanging out together so often? They are defining characteristics of Christianity. Actually, there are five—faith, hope, love, joy, and peace. These set us apart from the rest of the world. These mark us as different. Nonbelievers have no faith. They live without hope. They cannot love as God loves. They cannot experience real biblical joy. And no matter how many self-help books and yoga lessons they take, their hearts will never know true peace. We are given these things as gifts, and we ought to celebrate their presence in our souls.

*3. Those are the only two verses in which faith, hope, and love make an appearance together. But it is amazing how many times we can catch two out of three.*

• What reputation had the church in Colosse gained, according to Colossians 1:4?

_____

_____

• How does Paul describe the faith and love of his readers in 2 Thessalonians 1:3?

_____

_____

• What are we urged to pursue, according to 2 Timothy 2:22?

_____

_____

We emphasize so often that our salvation is a free gift, that we deemphasize the exhortations throughout the New Testament toward godly living. Many of us prefer to think of these commands as optional, extracurricular, bonus points. Paul obviously expected believers to live holy lives, be useful to God, and exercise their spiritual gifts. And it wasn't a way of life that just happened at salvation. Notice Paul's urgent words—"Flee" lusts and "pursue" righteousness. If you want to be good at anything, it takes commitment and practice. Becoming a mature believer is truly a "work of faith."

*4. Here's a smattering of verses that give us some idea of how faith and love interact in our lives. Match them up.*

___ 2 Corinthians 8:7      a. Love comes from a sincere faith.

___ Galatians 5:6          b. Paul prays that peace, love, and faith will be ours.

___ Ephesians 3:17         c. Faith, working through love, avails much.

___ Ephesians 6:23     d. Faith and love are in Christ Jesus.

___ 1 Thessalonians 3:6     e. Christ dwells in our hearts through faith.

___ 1 Timothy 1:5     f. We can abound (among other things) in faith and love.

___ 1 Timothy 1:14     g. Follow the pattern laid for us in faith and love.

___ 2 Timothy 1:13     h. Paul rejoiced over news of faith and love in the church.

## Did You Know?

*The letters we've been turning to quite a bit here—1 and 2 Timothy and Titus—are known as Pastoral Epistles. They were the very last of Paul's letters. He was martyred not long after he wrote them. They're called "pastoral" letters because he's writing to Timothy and Titus, and both were young pastors overseeing congregations of believers. In them, Paul gives his dear friends some parting admonitions about the responsibilities of leadership and about personal integrity.*

5. **Interestingly enough, if you allow patience to stand in for hope, there are a few more verses that mention our famous trio.**

- What notable character traits did Paul urge young Timothy to pursue in 1 Timothy 6:11?

_____

_____

● Paul urged Titus to teach the members of his congregation to cultivate what character qualities, according to Titus 2:2?

_____

_____

● What items were considered praiseworthy in the letter from Christ found in Revelation 2:19?

_____

_____

In the original Greek, the word translated "pursue" (1 Tim. 6:11; 2 Tim. 2:22) literally means to hunt or chase after an object, like a hunter chasing his prey. Back in Bible times, the hunters couldn't just climb up into their deer blinds and sip coffee while waiting to pick off a nice buck. They were working with arrows and even spears—sounds pretty prehistoric, huh? So when they hit their mark, they couldn't sit back and congratulate themselves. Those little roebucks kept right on running, and the hunter had no choice but to hotfoot it after them. They had to outlast the panicked deer until it weakened and fell. Paul uses this same idea in relationship to righteousness. "Chase it!" he says. Urgently, aggressively, as if your life—or at least your next meal—depends on it!

*6. What does Paul pray for believers in 2 Thessalonians 3:5?*

_____

_____

_____

_____

_____

_____

God directs us. In 2 Thessalonians 3:5, the word for "direct" literally means to open up the way by removing obstacles. We can take this two different ways. God is removing obstacles from our paths—things that might hinder us. This would be in the area of spiritual warfare, when the Spirit is actively protecting us. But the way that is being opened up can also be found in our own hearts. God is at work, convicting and cleansing, removing those obstacles in our lives that prevent us from following after Him. In this way He directs us into firm faith, godly love, and eternal hope in Jesus.

## PRAYING GOD'S PROMISES

Faith, hope, and love. They are the evidence of God's intimate touch on our hearts. Today's Scripture prayer, which is based on Hebrews 6:10–12, talks about all three—but mostly about love.

*God of Love, You have shown love to me. I know love because of You. You stir my heart with Your own love for other Christians. I like to do little things for them. I like to find ways to share Your love. I can see the light of love it brings to their eyes in response. Oh, nobody notices everything I do, but that doesn't matter. You know, Lord, and it's for You I'm doing it anyhow. Keep my heart soft, and keep giving me ideas on how to be loving. Every fresh inspiration is like an answer to prayer, and it bolsters up my faith. I want to keep right on doing so long as life lasts. Don't allow me to slip into indifference or selfishness. Direct me steadily on into love. I will continue in this way until my hope of all hopes is realized. Then I'll be able to tell You how much I love You face to face. Amen.*

One good passage on love deserves another. For today's Scripture prayer, read through these very familiar verses from the Love Chapter. As you journal below, find ways to personalize the descriptions of love and make them your prayer.

_____

_____

_____

_____

_____

*Love never gives up. Love cares more for others than for self. Love doesn't want what it doesn't have. Love doesn't strut, doesn't have a swelled head, doesn't force itself on others, isn't always "me first," doesn't fly off the handle, doesn't keep score of the sins of others, doesn't revel when others grovel, takes pleasure in the flowering of truth, puts up with anything, trusts God always, always looks for the best, never looks back, but keeps going to the end.*

1 Corinthians 13:4–7 MSG

## DAY TWO

# THE PATIENCE OF HOPE

*"Remembering without ceasing your. . .
patience of hope in our Lord Jesus Christ."*
1 Thessalonians 1:3 NKJV

I often listen to our local public radio station. The music thrills and soothes me, and I appreciate their informative, documentary-style news programs. One evening, with a half hour to myself in the car, I caught a program called "The Schickele Mix". Peter Schickele's premise is that all music is created equally, so he plays a decidedly eclectic range of music. In sharing his love of music with listeners, he passes along all manner of informative tidbits along with his opinions. On the night I listened in, he was doing a celebration of child prodigies—very young people who were capable of masterful musicianship. The question that Mr. Schickele raised was this—can a child, genius though they may be, really interpret the emotion of the music they play? To test this query, he had unearthed three recordings of a famous violinist. In each, he had performed the same solo. One was recorded when he was sixteen, another when he was middle-aged, and the last when he was getting rather old. Could we, the audience, guess which sample was played by the sixteen-year-old phenom, and which was the age-mellowed virtuoso? Do you know, we could tell! And the thing that gave it away was the violinist's patience. As a youngster, he had been note-perfect, but as this great musician had grown older and more experienced, he'd learned not to rush. He lingered over the notes, lending his playing a richer quality, and deeper, more poignant emotion.

Is there a lesson here for our spiritual lives? But, of course! We are not fully mature when we accept Christ in our hearts. We learn and we grow. Our spiritual gifts are nurtured through our experiences. And our relationship with the Lord changes with each passing year. It all takes time.

*1. James knew the value of patience. What does it produce in one's spiritual life, according to James 1:3, 4?*

*You know that when your faith succeeds in facing such trials, the result is the ability to endure. Make sure that your endurance carries you all the way without failing, so that you may be perfect and complete, lacking nothing.*

James 1:3, 4 NASB

When a baby is born, we cannot help but make sure that it is perfect. We count each little finger and each tiny toe. When James 1:4 says, "that you may be perfect and complete," the word complete is derived from a Greek all of its parts." Trials and testing are a reality of life. They reveal the nature of our faith. What's more, James assures us that they will produce patience. The Greek word for "produces" here means "to work its way down." So when our faith is tested, the experience works its way down into our hearts. We learn how to respond. We maintain a proper attitude. And over the course of time, patience has its perfect work in us. We will be complete.

2. *Patience doesn't come easy. Waiting isn't easy. How does wise old King Solomon describe the waiting process in Proverbs 13:12?*

_____

_____

_____

_____

_____

_____

_____

_____

3. *What does Romans 15:4 say God has placed into our hands in order to strengthen the patience of our hope?*

_____

_____

_____

_____

_____

_____

Patience here is literally "perseverance." The Scriptures enable us to persevere in the faith. They help us to hold on to hope. When we run into rough spots, it is God's Word that reminds us to be steadfast. When we begin to feel overwhelmed, it is our Bible that reminds us that the Lord has promised to be with us and to help us. When we apply ourselves earnestly to studying the Scriptures, our weak areas will be shored up, and our faith will be strengthened. We'll be able to persevere. . .patiently.

## 4. Learning to be patient often means learning to wait.

Psalm 52:9—In the _____ of Your _____
I will _____ on Your _____,
for it is _____.

Psalm 59:9—I will _____ for _____,
O You his_____.

Isaiah 8:17—I will _____ on the _____
. . . And I will _____ in Him.

Micah 7:7—I will _____ to the _____;
I will _____ for the _____
of my _____; My God will _____ me.

"I will wait for You." "I will wait on Your name." What is meant by waiting on the Lord? As this phrase is used throughout the Old Testament, it conveys two ideas. One is endurance—that would be patience. The other is expectancy—that would be hope. We endure through life's trials because we know it's worth it. We hang in there patiently because we know it pleases God. We persevere because something deep down inside us tells us that it's the right thing to do. We persist for just one more day because we know that some day, the wait will be over. It could be any day now. It could be today!

## 5. Sometimes we are the ones who must be patient. At other times, God's own patience seems to flow through us. Either way, patience always bears good fruit in our lives.

- What did David do, and what was the Lord's response, according to Psalm 40:1?

_____

_____

- In Luke 8:15, part of Jesus' parable of the sower, what part does patience play in the process?

  _____

  _____

- According to Colossians 1:11, what does God do on our behalf so that we can display patience with joy?

  _____

  _____

*6. What does James compare our hope and patient waiting to in James 5:7, 8?*

_____

_____

_____

_____

_____

_____

_____

We hope while we wait. When we wait patiently, we're being grown up into maturity. And as we persevere, our lives begin to bear good fruit.

## PRAYING GOD'S PROMISES

That last section from James seems to sum up our waiting for the fulfillment of our hopes so well—let's use James 5:7–11 here as the basis for today's Scripture Prayer.

*Rest in the LORD, and wait patiently for Him; do not fret because of him who prospers in his way, because of the man who brings wicked schemes to pass. Cease from anger, and forsake wrath; do not fret—it only causes harm. For evildoers shall be cut off; but those who wait on the LORD, they shall inherit the earth. For yet a little while and the wicked shall be no more; indeed, you will look carefully for his place, but it shall be no more. But the meek shall inherit the earth, and shall delight themselves in the abundance of peace.*

Psalm 37:7–11 NKJV

*Coming King, help me to be patient. I know You're coming, but I don't know when. Give me the patience of a farmer. When he plants a seed, he can only wait. He must trust You for the rains that nourish and strengthen it. He knows the harvest will come when the time is just right. Make me patient. Help me to persevere. Establish my heart. And, Lord, in the meantime, help me not to grumble so much. I would hate to be caught cranky and ranting at the very moment You walked through the door. Temper my moods, and help me to follow Your example of meekness. There have been those who belonged to You—like the prophets—who had to endure real suffering. They met hardships with patience for Your sake. Indeed, You blessed them for it. They faced difficulties without ever knowing the reasons why. I want to be more like that. Teach me to depend on Your sovereignty, Your mercy, and Your compassion. Amen.*

**Now you have a go at it.** Psalm 37 is a wonderful passage—one of my very favorites. Take its many exhortations to heart, and make them your prayer today.

# DAY THREE

# HOPE IS OUR ARMOR

*"Let us who are of the day be sober, putting on the breastplate of faith and love, and as a helmet the hope of salvation."*

1 Thessalonians 5:8 NKJV

We love the romantic tales of brave knights and fair ladies. We envision castles bright with flags and banners, drawbridges over moats, jousting tournaments, round tables, and gleaming suits of armor. Of course Paul wasn't thinking these things when he gave us his list of armor in 1 Thessalonians. The images in his mind were of Roman centurions and the foot soldiers of the great phalanxes. Everywhere that Paul went on his missionary journeys, he was well within the confines of the Roman Empire, so Roman soldiers were commonplace. Everyone knew what armor looked like, and so do we, for that matter. Movie-makers have duplicated it quite accurately. Just think of Charlton Heston in *Ben-Hur* or Russell Crowe in *Gladiator*. Even the little Martian in old Bugs Bunny cartoons wore the armor of a Roman soldier—if you leave out the sneakers, of course.

No matter its relative configuration, armor serves the same purpose throughout all of history. It protected its wearer from injury in battle. Each piece shielded a place of vulnerability. Good armor was strong, impenetrable. It turned aside arrows. Sword blows glanced off its surface. It guarded against the attacks of the enemy.

*1. Ah! Here is that familiar list of the armor of God. Fill in the blanks for each piece and part.*

*"Put on the whole armor of God, that you may be able to stand against the wiles of the devil. For we do not wrestle against flesh and blood, but against principalities, against powers, against the rulers of the darkness of this age, against spiritual hosts of wickedness in the heavenly places. Therefore take up the whole armor of God, that you may be able to withstand in the evil day, and having done all, to stand. Stand therefore, having girded your waist with*

*truth, having put on the breastplate of righteousness, and having shod your feet with the preparation of the gospel of peace; above all, taking the shield of faith with which you will be able to quench all the fiery darts of the wicked one. And take the helmet of salvation, and the sword of the Spirit, which is the word of God."* —Ephesians 6:11–17 NKJV

**Put on the Whole Armor of God**

The Belt of _____

The Breastplate of _____

The Footgear of _____

The Shield of _____

The Helmet of_____

The Sword of _____ which is the _____

*2. Why does Paul say we need this armor in that Ephesians passage? He names several different things from which it will protect us. What are they?*

_____

_____

_____

_____

_____

We know all about protection in this day and age. We have health insurance, life insurance, car insurance, home owner's insurance—to protect us against the unforeseen calamities of life. We take precautions for our personal protection—smoke detectors, seat belts, air bags, rubber gloves, defense classes, mace, first aid kits. We guard our stuff with passwords, PIN numbers, firewalls, car alarms, home security systems, fences, deadbolt locks, watchdogs. But the protection God offers isn't about earthly things. His armor protects us in spiritual confrontations—in the battles that take place in our hearts and minds.

*3.* **There is another list of armor in the Bible. Turn to Isaiah 59:17. What is the list of battle gear that the Lord Himself puts on here?**

Armor—the Kevlar vest of ancient times. It protects our soft spots, our vulnerable places, our areas of weakness. It keeps the injuries we receive from being fatal ones. Paul knew how much we would need to guard our thoughts, our feelings, our inclinations, our hearts. The armor of God—truth, faith, hope, preparation, righteous living, and the Word of God do just that.

*4.* **Before you can put your armor on, you have to take something off! What does Paul say we need to get rid of in Romans 13:12?**

> *The night is almost gone; the day of salvation will soon be here. So don't live in darkness. Get rid of your evil deeds. Shed them like dirty clothes. Clothe yourselves with the armor of right living, as those who live in the light.*
>
> Romans 13:12 NLT

I once heard a pastor draw a conclusion about the armor of God that made the whole congregation dissolve into laughter. He was making the point that we can't pick and choose the pieces of armor that we like while ignoring others. We need it all, or else we're left vulnerable. Then he said that too many Christians think that once they've been saved, they don't have to do anything else for the Lord. They're "in," and proceed to do just as they please with their lives. They don't care about truth or righteous living. They don't prepare themselves to spread the gospel. They don't bother with God's Word. You know what that makes them? Christian streakers—because they've grabbed the helmet of salvation, but they're not wearing anything else! Ha!

*5. God urges us to live in a way that defends us from spiritual attacks, but we can also rest in the assurance that He will be our Defender.*

- What does David say that God has given to him in Psalm 18:35?

- According to Psalm 28:7, what role has God taken in David's life?

- What do God's truths and faithful promises provide for those who trust them, according to Psalm 91:4?

Always remember just how personal God's watch-care over us is. God doesn't just give strength. God is our strength. God doesn't just provide a shield. He is our shield. He doesn't delegate our prayers. He doesn't forward us to His message center. He doesn't send in a stunt double. When we call on God, He takes care of us Himself.

*6. Take a look at this paraphrase of Deuteronomy 33:29. Try inserting your name into this verse in all the appropriate places. Is this how you feel about the Lord and His salvation?*

*Lucky Israel! Who has it as good as you? A people saved by God! The Shield who defends you, the Sword who brings triumph. Your enemies will come crawling on their bellies and you'll march on their backs. —Deuteronomy 33:29 MSG*

Do you really know how good you have it, or are you starting to take salvation for granted. Faith, hope, love, joy, and peace feel like old hat? Well, be thankful you don't have to try to live without them. God is our Defender, our Shield, our Sword. He has given us the hope of salvation as a helmet. Wear that hat with joy!

## Praying God's Promises

Today's Scripture Prayer is based on Psalm 84:8–12, in which God is celebrated as our Protector.

*Protector of My Soul, hear my prayer. God, You are my shield. I would rather spend one day in Your presence than have a thousand days to frivolously do as I please. I would rather be assigned a humble task in Your house—to hold the door for others coming to see You—than to live like a queen in her castle among the wicked. You are like the sun—blindingly bright in Your holy perfection. You are my Shield. I know You are taking care of me. Lord grant me grace. It is You who gives glory. You have promised to withhold no good thing from me, if I will only walk in Your ways. Make me an upright woman, full of grace and goodness. O, Lord of hosts, bless me when I put my trust in You. Amen.*

Read through the Ephesians passage here in the margin. It's our Armor of God passage in yet another translation. May it inspire fresh notions as you take the time to journal it as your personal prayer.

*Finally, be strong in the Lord and in his great power. Put on the full armor of God so that you can fight against the devil's evil tricks. Our fight is not against people on earth but against the rulers and authorities and the powers of this world's darkness, against the spiritual powers of evil in the heavenly world. That is why you need to put on God's full armor. Then on the day of evil you will be able to stand strong. And when you have finished the whole fight, you will still be standing. So stand strong, with the belt of truth tied around your waist and the protection of right living on your chest. On your feet wear the Good News of peace to help you stand strong. And also use the shield of faith with which you can stop all the burning arrows of the Evil One. Accept God's salvation as your helmet, and take the sword of the Spirit, which is the word of God.*

Ephesians 6:10–17 NCV

## DAY FOUR

# HOPE, AND OUR CROWN OF REJOICING

*"For what is our hope, or joy, or crown of rejoicing? Is it not even you in the presence of our Lord Jesus Christ at His coming?"*

1 Thessalonians 2:19 NKJV

Good things are . . . good, of course. But why settle for good when you can have something better. We'd all love to enjoy the better things in life. But is better enough, if we can trade up for the very best? Good to better. Better to best. We've reached the limit, haven't we? Perhaps not. From best, a few might press on to priceless. Priceless things are timeless, rare, and irreplaceable. They are the masterpieces. The pièce de résistance. The crowning joy of any collection.

Our own lives are filled with priceless moments. They are moments so perfect that nothing could be changed to make them better. To try to do so would be gilding the lily. These are the crowning moments, the Kodak moments we want to remember forever. Paul had an abundance of hardships in his career as a missionary and church planter, but he didn't dwell on them. He was too caught up in the memories of the crowning moments he had experienced along the way. To him, they were precious, priceless. They were his treasure. They were his pride and joy. And what were they? People. Each person who heard the message and became a believer. Each new follower of Christ. Each precious, priceless, irreplaceable soul that was granted eternal hope. Paul knew their names. He knew their faces. He called them his crown of rejoicing.

*1.* **Whose head shall bear a crown, according to Revelation 14:14?**

"Crown Him with many crowns." "Bring forth the royal diadem." It is easy to think of crowns where the Lord is concerned. It's altogether appropriate for the King of kings and Lord of lords to wear the symbol of His authority. But often the Scriptures talk about crowning moments—times of abundant blessing, or things that elevate an already good life to an extraordinary one.

*2.* **Match up these crowning moments from the Scriptures.**

___ Psalm 21:3     a. Wisdom crowns its possessor with grace and glory.

___ Psalm 65:11     b. The Lord will be a crown of glory to His people.

___ Proverbs 4:9     c. An excellent wife is a crown to her husband.

___ Proverbs 12:4     d. The year is crowned by a bountiful harvest.

___ Proverbs 16:31     e. The silver-haired head is a crown of glory.

___ Proverbs 17:6     f. We are crowned by blessings of goodness from God.

___ Isaiah 28:5     g. Grandchildren are the crown of their grandparents.

At other times in the New Testament, the crown refers to the prize we are striving to win. It is the goal, the trophy, the blue ribbon, the reward, the honor we receive once we cross the finish line.

*3. Paul is the one we usually think of when we talk about obtaining a crown, but other writers refer to it as well.*

- What is the quality of the crown for which we compete, according to 1 Corinthians 9:25?

- Who will receive the crown of life, according to James 1:12?

- When does Peter say we shall receive the crown of glory in 1 Peter 5:4?

- And what will be the end of all our tribulations, according to Revelation 2:10?

Hope affects how we look at others. We who have been given hope have a God-given longing to see others gain that same hope. Every person is loved by God. Every person is facing eternal life. We want to get the message to them. Paul knew the joy of being the bearer of Good News and of seeing hope dawn on the faces of new believers.

**4.** *What does the Word say about this gospel that brings such hope and about the ones who carry it to others?*

- How does Paul describe the gospel of Christ in Romans 1:16?

  _____

  _____

- What did Paul ask people to pray on his behalf, according to Ephesians 6:19?

  _____

  _____

- Did Paul have a hit-and-run delivery of the gospel? What does 1 Thessalonians 2:8 say?

  _____

  _____

Paul stayed for months and even years at a time in the cities where he planted churches. He worked side by side with new believers. He met with them to teach and disciple them almost daily. The ties of their friendships were strong by the time he moved on. He called these sons and daughters in the faith his crowning joy. He was like a proud papa! And Paul couldn't wait for the day when he could go into the presence of the Lord, surrounded by all the men and women he had led to Him. That was to be the absolute crowning jewel!

**5.** *In what ways did Paul let the brethren know he loved them? Take a look at these excerpts from his letters!*

- How often do we say, "I wish I were there!" What does Paul say in Colossians 2:5?

  _____

  _____

- What does Paul call his fellow believers in Philippians 4:1?

- How does Paul "brag on" his sons and daughters in the faith in 2 Corinthians 1:14?

Are you starting to get the picture that people matter? Everything we work for in this world—houses, cars, clothes, shoes, hobbies—will one day be gone. The only thing we can take with us into eternity are those we have led to the Lord. Have you ever looked at the people in your congregation, your Sunday school class, or your Bible study in quite this way before?

*6. Paul is so full of encouragement for his sons and daughters in the faith. Take a look at these "sweet nothings" and terms of endearment! Do you have friends in the faith that you talk to this way?*

- What does Paul call believers in 1 Corinthians 9:2?

- What does Paul call the brethren in 2 Corinthians 3:2, 3?

- What does 1 Thessalonians 2:20 call Paul's sons and daughters in the faith?

*You are our epistle written in our hearts, known and read by all men; clearly you are an epistle of Christ, ministered by us, written not with ink but by the Spirit of the living God, not on tablets of stone but on tablets of flesh, that is, of the heart.*

2 Corinthians 3:2, 3 NKJV

The hope that we carry in our hearts is a hope that we can share with others. Those people we lead to the Lord will become jewels in our crowns in heaven. People are the only things that will carry on after this old world is gone. They're more important than anything else. So invest your time, your friendship, your gifts, and your love in the people around you. Let your brothers and sisters in the faith be your crowning joy!

### PRAYING GOD'S PROMISES

We hang on to hope. We persevere with patience. We run the race with endurance. This is how our life is described. Today's prayer is based on Hebrews 11:1–3, which urges all of us to run the race set before us.

*Giver of Crowns, Help me to run this race with endurance. I need to lighten my load. No burdens to weigh me down, no sins to trip me up. I am looking at what You have set before me. Most of my responsibilities are clear. Help me to take care of them with faithfulness. Help me to endure, even when the job gets wearisome. Let me lift my eyes off of my own selfishness and restlessness and focus instead on Jesus. The things He endured were terrible—spitefulness, hatred, pain, and shame. But He made it through! He endured, and that inspires me to hang in there. Don't let weariness or discouragement hamper me on this race. Keep me close to Jesus. It is He who will help me to finish. Amen.*

**Now it is your turn.** Your text today is 1 Corinthians 9:24–27. This is Paul's pep talk for the race. Take it to heart, and make it your prayer.

*Do you not know that those who run in a race all run, but one receives the prize? Run in such a way that you may obtain it. And everyone who competes for the prize is temperate in all things. Now they do it to obtain a perishable crown, but we for an imperishable crown. Therefore I run thus: not with uncertainty. Thus I fight: not as one who beats the air. But I discipline my body and bring it into subjection, lest, when I have preached to others, I myself should become disqualified.*

1 Corinthians 9:24–27 NKJV

## DAY FIVE

## A LIFE OF HOPE

*"Blessed are those who trust in the LORD and have made the LORD their hope and confidence."*
Jeremiah 17:7 NLT

What would it be like if your whole future was determined by the day of the week on which you were born?

> Monday's child is fair of face,
> Tuesday's child is full of grace,
> Wednesday's child is full of woe,
> Thursday's child has far to go,
> Friday's child is loving and giving,
> Saturday's child works hard for a living,
> and the child who is born on Sunday
> is fair and wise and good and gay.
>
> —Mother Goose

Not a very pretty prospect, if you don't like the future you're allotted. Thankfully, this little nursery rhyme is better poetry than prediction. Our lives are more like the serials that were so very popular back around the turn of the century. Such stories regaled the reader with exciting stories of adventure, discovery, and rags-to-riches heroics. The characters were always getting into one scrape after another, and just when the plot thickened and the situation reached a climax, there would be three little words printed at the bottom of the page—"to be continued." And the continuing adventures of so-and-so would resume in the next issue.

Have you ever read a story that was so good, you wished it would never end? Well, that's the very kind of serial you're in right now! Our own lives are a continuing saga. We may not go to sea or discover the tomb of an ancient Egyptian king, but we have our own series of cliff hangers. Life's a continuing thing—it goes on. It's a never-ending story of faith and hope and love. No matter what happens, for better or for worse, we can—we must—continue on.

*1. What does the psalmist say that he will do continually, according to Psalm 71:14?*

Continue. Persist. Remain. Persevere. Keep on. Advance. Forge ahead. Go on. Keep at it. Hang in. Hang on. Last. Maintain. Make headway. Move ahead. Pursue. Push on. Run on. Don't stop. Stick to it. Stay on the job. Keep your hand on the plow. Keep your nose to the grindstone. Steady as she goes. Keep on truckin'. Onward! Further up and further in!

*2. What facts help David to persevere and continue to hope in the Lord?*

- Psalm 71:3

● Psalm 73:23

_____

_____

Continuing can be hard work. It can become routine, feel like a rut, and give you the sensation of going nowhere. Continuing might mean enduring just one day more, in spite of the discouragement, in spite of the pain. But the bright side to continuing is that we serve a God who is continual. He's always been and always will be. He's not subject to fluctuations in mood or opinion. He never changes, never lies, and never fails. So we can take courage in knowing that we can continually return to the Lord for His help, and He will be there for us every time.

_3._ **What beautiful promise is given to us in Isaiah 58:11? Fill in these blanks.**

The _____ will _____ you _____, and _____ your _____ in drought, And _____ your bones; You shall be like a _____ _____, and like a _____ of _____ whose _____ do not _____.
—Isaiah 58:11 NKJV

We often associate the idea of endurance with pain and discomfort. We see in our mind's eye a grueling, survivalist obstacle course, with one staggering challenge following another. Sweat pours off the contestants as they push themselves beyond all physical limits. We see their exhaustion. We see them fall by the wayside, one after another. We see the bitterness of defeat. A few hardy souls might rise to such a challenge, but most of us find the picture intimidating. We shrink at the thought. That's why I love this Isaiah passage. Yes, we have to continue, to persevere in the ways of the Lord. But we're not going it alone. The Lord is beside us, holding our hand, guiding us along. This race may challenge us, but it will also strengthen us. God does not push us to the ends of our abilities, but helps and nourishes us along the way. We won't end up collapsing at the finish. We will come forth as beautifully as a watered garden.

*4. There are many examples throughout Scripture of things which were done continually. Match them up!*

___ Psalm 34:1          a. I will serve God continually.

___ Psalm 119:44       b. The Lord's praises shall be continually
                          in my mouth.

___ Proverbs 6:21      c. I will wait on the Lord continually.

___ Daniel 6:16        d. Continually offer the sacrifice of praise.

___ Hosea 12:6         e. The apostles gave their time
                          continually to the word and prayer.

___ Acts 6:4           f. I will keep the Law of the Lord
                          continually.

___ Hebrews 13:15      g. I will have God's Word bound continu-
                          ally on my heart.

*5. One of the jobs of the apostles was to encourage believers in their faith, strengthening their hope, and enabling them to continue living for the Lord.*

● What did Paul urge believers to continue in, according to Colossians 4:2?

_____

_____


● According to 1 Timothy 2:15, what were women to continue in?

_____

_____

• What did the writer of Hebrews say should be continued, according to Hebrews 13:1?

_____

_____

• What encouragement did the disciples receive, as we find it in Acts 14:22?

_____

_____

• What did Paul urge Timothy to continue in? Read 2 Timothy 3:14.

_____

_____

*6. And what is the promise for which we most hope? Look in Psalm 49:9.*

_____

_____

_____

_____

_____

_____

_____

_____

_____

Continue in a life of hope. Continue to hang on to hope. And when we see our hope at last, we will continue on, right into eternity!

## PRAYING GOD'S PROMISES

The Book of Psalms is like a hymnbook, for all of the poems we find there were put to music or spoken while music played in the background. Today's prayer is based on Psalm 84:1–3.

*My Rock, I love You with all my strength. You are my mountain. You are my castle. You are my rescuer. You are my God. You are my strength. I trust You completely. You are my shield. You are the power that saves me. You are my stronghold. When I am in need, I will call on no one but You. Only You are able to answer. Only You are worthy of praise. Amen.*

Now here is another psalm of David—and a very familiar one at that. The Twenty-third Psalm gives us a beautiful picture of God continuing with us as we journey through life. He's taking care of us, and we are trusting Him. Make David's poem your prayer today as you journal it below.

*The LORD is my shepherd; I shall not want. He makes me to lie down in green pastures; He leads me beside the still waters. He restores my soul; He leads me in the paths of righteousness For His name's sake. Yea, though I walk through the valley of the shadow of death, I will fear no evil; for You are with me; Your rod and Your staff, they comfort me. You prepare a table before me in the presence of my enemies; You anoint my head with oil; My cup runs over. Surely goodness and mercy shall follow me all the days of my life; And I will dwell in the house of the LORD forever.*

Psalm 23:1–6 NKJV

## CONCLUSION

Our hope is abounding! How could it not be after everything we have learned this week. We know that faith, hope, and love—along with joy and peace—are ours. We have seen how hope protects us, like armor. We have been reminded of how precious each person's life is, and understand why Paul called his converts his "crown of rejoicing." We have explored the patience of hope—waiting, yes, but maturing along the way. And we have considered the continuing life of hope. We persevere in hope, with God at our side the whole way. What a week of encouragement—but the best is yet to come. Next week we'll finally lay out just what it is we're hoping for!

### JOURNALING SUGGESTIONS

*1.* **Take a likely psalm—one that uses the words "shelter" and "refuge" quite a bit. Then substitute the word "hope" in their places. Read the new version out loud. Does it make hope come alive in a new way?**

_____

_____

_____

_____

_____

_____

_____

_____

_____

*2.* **How many things can you think of that take practice to get good at it. Make a good, long list. Now consider. If all these things take time and effort in order to gain proficiency, why do we expect our Christian walk to just "happen"?**

_____

_____

_____

_____

_____

_____

*3. Why is waiting so hard? Why is being patient so difficult? Why does something that feels like doing nothing have to be the path to maturity?*

_____

_____

_____

_____

_____

_____

_____

_____

*4. The Christian faith is often compared to farming. How many ways can you think of that make it such an appropriate analogy?*

_____

_____

_____

_____

_____

_____

_____

*5. If Christianity was an episode of "Survivor," what would the challenges be? What purposes would they serve? What lessons would they teach? (Have fun with this one.)*

_____

_____

_____

_____

### JOURNALING QUOTE

*I write my thoughts on what's happening in my life. I write thoughts on what's happening in other people's lives. Sometimes I write other people's thoughts on what's happening in my life! The main thing is I'm writing, and when you are writing, you are thinking and feeling. You are processing, you are working things out.*

Nicole Johnson

# LESSON 5

# THE HOPE OF GLORY

*"Looking for the blessed hope and glorious appearing of our great God and Savior Jesus Christ"*

Titus 2:13 NKJV

## INTRODUCTION BY PATSY CLAIRMONT

Glory; the mega butterfly of faith. . .like attempting to net a distant Monarch in flight when we try to capture glory, it flutters just out of reach. "Raise the veil," we cry, longing to get just a peek into eternity, but, alas, it is appointed unto man once to die and then. . .glory. So we pace and ponder. Gratefully the Scriptures give us just enough preview that our hearts crowd with anticipation as we tap our toe and sing, "I've got a home in glory land that out shines the sun. . ."

Glory land. . .imagine, which is what we must do if we are to touch even the hem of heaven, a place filled with God's glory. Have you ever thought about the word "glory"? What exactly is it? Words like holy, light, and powerful come to mind and they should, for glory is that and more. It is pure, purging, and perfect. And it is fearsome. Huh? Remember Moses on the mountainside? When God's glory passed by, God covered Moses' face not to deny him a thrilling experience, but He was protecting Moses from something he wasn't prepared to handle. Moses could not have survived exposure to God's full glory, nor can we as long as we are bound in these earth suits. Humanity and divinity are as far apart as heaven and earth. And if you haven't measured that lately, trust me, it's a far piece. Come take my hand and let's at least imagine the hope of glory together. . .

Pressing our noses to the windows in Scripture we see streets of pure gold, like transparent glass, a city that has no need for the sun or moon to shine, for the glory of God illuminates it. Its gates are always open, and there is no night. There is a pure river of water of life, clear as crystal, for the thirsty, proceeding from the throne of God and of the Lamb. The tree of life is there for the healing of the nations. God wipes away every tear; there shall be no more death, nor sorrow, nor crying, no more pain.

Whoa, talk about a future. Hope pulsates in every description, filling us with awe and wonder.

Enter these pages with expectancy as we learn that irrepressible hope goes beyond today, and tomorrow it goes into glory.

This week, we'll answer the question, "What are we hoping for?" The short answer is—life! New life. Sinless life. Holy life. Glorified life. Eternal life. We shall be changed. We shall be complete. We shall see our Savior face-to-face. We shall dwell in God's presence. Is it any wonder that the writers of Scripture spoke with such earnestness, such eagerness, such anticipation of Jesus' return? We join all of creation in groaning, "How much longer, Lord?"

## A PEEK AT OUR WEEK

- **Day One:** All Creation Waits
- **Day Two:** Justified, Sanctified, Glorified!
- **Day Three:** How Long, Lord!
- **Day Four:** Face-to-Face
- **Day Five:** Death Has No Sting

## DAY ONE

# ALL CREATION WAITS

*"Everything God made is waiting with excitement for God to show his children's glory completely."*

Romans 8:19 NCV

I've often thought it would be a glorious thing to have a manicure. Just think—all ten of my fingernails trimmed and buffed and shimmering with polish. A matched set—elegant, sophisticated, trés chic. There's a very good reason that this sounds so glorious to me. Reality is much more prosaic. You see, I actually use my hands. They are exposed to an incredible variety of substances during any given day. My hands get red and rough, and I have to scrape the crud out from under my nails. Bread dough, Play-Doh®, scouring powder, peanut butter, brownie batter, craft glue, diaper ointment, dirt. I'm forever breaking a nail. There are rips, chips, snags, and rough spots. If I want to take my nails out for an evening, I haul out my basket of nail polish bottles. Clip, file, buff, and basecoat. Then carefully, ever so slowly, the first coat goes on. Concentrate. Stay inside the lines. So far so good. But as the second coat is being applied, disaster inevitably strikes. This nail is smudged. That nail has the waffle pattern of fabric pressed into it. One has the fingerprint of its neighbor firmly stamped across the tip. Clumps, scrapes, streaks, scuff marks, and brush marks happen. If I try to use nail polish remover on just one irreparably damaged nail, half the polish will disappear off of two perfectly good nails in the process. So out comes the basecoat, and we start all over again. Yes, there are days when I long for a perfectly manicured set of nails.

All of us long for perfection. And in this world, things always fall just short. We get glimpses of glory, breathtaking moments of joy. But they are only a foretaste. The real deal is just ahead. It's what we're hoping for. And we're not alone. All of creation is waiting with us.

*1.* **We are not alone in our longing. What is creation waiting for, according to Romans 8:19–22?**

_____

_____

_____

_____

_____

_____

_____

_____

_____

_____

_____

_____

_____

_____

_____

> *For the earnest expectation of the creation eagerly waits for the revealing of the sons of God. For the creation was subjected to futility, not willingly, but because of Him who subjected it in hope; because the creation itself also will be delivered from the bondage of corruption into the glorious liberty of the children of God. For we know that the whole creation groans and labors with birth pangs together until now.*
>
> Romans 8:19–22 NKJV

Creation waits "for the revealing of the sons of God." How about that—our own cheering section! Of course, it's not just rooting for us. The earth was subjected to the curse at the same time we were. "Cursed is the ground for your sake" (Gen. 3:17 NKJV). As lovely as our world can be, all is not as it should be. It may sound strange to think of our whole planet groaning under the weight of sin, but it's no stranger than the fact that all of creation shares our eagerness to see Jesus return. He will put things right.

## Did You Know?

*People did not soon forget the consequences of the curse. It affected their everyday lives as they farmed the land. Even after hundreds of years, it remained common knowledge. In Genesis 5:29, Noah's parents remembered the source of their toil and looked forward in hope of finding peace and rest. "He called his name Noah, saying, 'This one will comfort us concerning our work and the toil of our hands, because of the ground which the LORD has cursed'" (NKJV). Noah's name characterized the hope of men. It meant rest, peace, quiet, and comfort.*

*2.* **The psalms are filled with expressions of anticipation and hope. David keenly felt his soul's longing for God. Paul was no less eager.**

● To what does David compare his longing for God in Psalm 143:6?

_____

_____

● For what does Paul wait eagerly, according to 1 Corinthians 1:7?

_____

_____

● What is the ultimate desire of David, according to Psalm 17:15?

_____

_____

There is a part of our innermost heart that will always be dissatisfied. Beautiful things only pique its appetite. Good things only make it yearn for something more. Joyful occasions leave it wondering, "Is that all?" This restless discontentment has often been described as our soul's homesickness for heaven. We join David in saying, "I shall be satisfied when I awake in Your likeness" (Ps. 17:15 NKJV).

*3. One of the most wonderful things about our Bible is that it tells how everything will end. The plot may have a few twists ahead, but God doesn't leave any loose ends. What do we find lifted in Revelation 22:3?*

_____

_____

_____

_____

_____

_____

_____

_____

_____

This is a Hope with a capital H! The end of sin. The lifting of the curse. And it will all come about when another Hope is fulfilled. The revelation of Jesus Christ. He's coming back, you know. It will be the ultimate return of the King.

*4. How do we know Jesus is coming back? Now, that's a fair question. Let's answer it.*

• What did Jesus Himself say was coming after His death, according to Mark 14:62?

_____

_____

- What did the angels tell the crowd who had gathered to witness Jesus' Ascension in Acts 1:11?

  _____

  _____

- Later on, Paul lays out the sequence of events for us. What is his version of the story, recorded in 1 Thessalonians 4:17?

  _____

  _____

Over and over, throughout the Book of Revelation, Jesus says, "Behold. I am coming quickly!" Some translations use the word "soon." "I am coming soon." Quickly seems to imply the suddenness of Christ's return. Soon implies that the time is near. Either word is fine, so long as we understand the imminent nature of the Second Coming. It could be any time now.

*5. What did Jesus tell us about His own return? Only that He would come unexpectedly and that He would come soon. Take a look at these verses from Revelation. They each hold a warning and a promise.*

Revelation 3:11—Behold, I am coming quickly! _____ what you have, that no one may _____ your _____.

Revelation 22:7—Behold, I am coming quickly! _____ is he who _____ the _____ of the _____ of this _____.

Revelation 22:12—Behold, I am coming quickly, and My _____ _____ is with Me, to _____ to _____ according to his _____.

Revelation 22:20—He who testifies to these things says, "_____ _____ I am _____ _____." Amen. Even so, _____, _____!

What are the last words you say to someone dear, right before you are parted? What are the last words you close with in a letter, just before signing your name? What are the last words your children hear from your lips each night before they go to sleep? The very last words of Christ recorded in our Bibles are right there in Revelation 22:20. He wants us to know that He's coming back. He shall return. And His coming will be soon.

*6. How do we know that Jesus' coming is soon? What do we know about His appearing?*

- What will be the state of the world when Jesus returns, according to Matthew 24:37?

- When does Matthew 24:44 say that Jesus will come?

- To what is Jesus' return compared in Matthew 24:27?

- What analogy is used of the coming of Christ in Matthew 24:38, 39?

All creation waits for the final fulfillment of the prophecy of Scripture. We know that one day, sin will be done away with. We know that the curse will be lifted from the earth. We have been told that Jesus is coming back, though we don't know when. All we need to know is that these promises are true, they could happen at any time, and their occurrence will bring about the fulfillment of every hope.

*The created world itself can hardly wait for what's coming next. Everything in creation is being more or less held back. God reins it in until both creation and all the creatures are ready and can be released at the same moment into the glorious times ahead. Meanwhile, the joyful anticipation deepens. All around us we observe a pregnant creation. The difficult times of pain throughout the world are simply birth pangs. But it's not only around us; it's within us. The Spirit of God is arousing us within. We're also feeling the birth pangs. These sterile and barren bodies of ours are yearning for full deliverance. That is why waiting does not diminish us, any more than waiting diminishes a pregnant mother. We are enlarged in the waiting. We, of course, don't see what is enlarging us. But the longer we wait, the larger we become, and the more joyful our expectancy.*

Romans 8:19–25 MSG

## PRAYING GOD'S PROMISES

The New Testament epistles are filled with encouragements to hang in there until the coming of Christ. Whatever we might be asked to endure in this world will be exchanged for blessings from God's hand. Today's prayer is based on Peter's words in 1 Peter 1:7, 8, 13.

*Returning Lord, prove my faith. When trials, big and small, seem to interfere with my plans, give me the perspective to see them for what they are. Help me to take them in stride. Make them opportunities that I make the most of—opportunities for me to show You that I trust You. Strengthen my faith. Purify it like gold in the fire. You say that my faith is precious to You, so I want to have more of it! Make me strong in Your strength so that You can receive all praise, glory, and honor in my life. Meanwhile, my soul is breathless with anticipation. Your coming is soon. I will see You for myself! I know I have never seen You, but I trust You and I love You. My heart is filled with a glorious, inexpressible joy at the thought of coming face to face with my Lord. Do come quickly! I will be ready. Amen.*

**Now it is your turn.** Use a little creativity and transform this passage from Romans into your own prayer of earnest expectation.

# DAY TWO

# JUSTIFIED, SANCTIFIED, GLORIFIED!

*"Therefore, having been justified by faith, we have peace
with God through our Lord Jesus Christ, through whom also we
have access by faith into this grace in which we stand, and rejoice
in hope of the glory of God."*

Romans 5:1, 2 NKJV

The other day, I asked my kindergartener to tidy up our family room. I was passing by with an armload of dishtowels for the kitchen, and noticing the scattering of Legos on the floor, threw a quick word of admonition over my shoulder. "Look at that mess! Put away the Legos now, please." I returned to my sorting and folding, and the child grudgingly began to pick up. Not much later, I peeked in to see if the job had been done properly. For a moment, I was flabbergasted. There sat the cherubic boy, looking at a picture book, surrounded by a scattering of toys. "I asked you to clean up in here," I said with pointed displeasure. "I did," came the innocent reply. "I picked up all the Legos." With silent amusement, I scanned the floor. Sure enough. He had taken the time to sift through all the jumbled toys on the floor, and he had put away every single Lego. All that was left were wooden blocks, toy cars, and a few hand puppets. He had taken my words too literally. Giving more specific instructions, I set him to finishing the task more thoroughly.

I admire a thorough job—one which leaves no thing undone. A thorough job of packing doesn't leave the toothbrush at home. A thorough job of ironing doesn't leave one wrinkle. A thorough job of cleaning doesn't leave one speck of dust. When God decided to obliterate the sin that crept into the world at the Fall, He took the time to make a thorough job of it. Christ's sacrifice was necessary to ensure that all sin could be dealt with—past, present, and future. Our future hope of a sinless existence is how the story will end. But it is worthwhile to consider just how effectively God countered the enemy's strategies in order to give us this hope.

*1.* **When we are justified, the sins of our past are forgiven.**

- What does Romans 3:28 clearly state as our means of justification?

  _____

  _____

- Having been justified, what does Romans 5:1 say we now have?

  _____

  _____

- While faith provides us a means of justification, what does Romans 5:9 say is our source of justification?

  _____

  _____

"Justified," as it is used in the New Testament, is actually a term borrowed from the legal profession. There are so many television programs set in the courtroom these days, we've all picked up a little bit of the lingo. Let's borrow some of it. We were brought up on charges of sin and stood accused before the Judge. There was no way we could make bail, because our crime mandated a death sentence. But before our hearing could be concluded, the courtroom doors burst open, and someone brings shocking new evidence before the Judge. Jesus is willing to post bail so that we can go free. Not only that, He's willing to stand in our place and serve our sentence for us. He'll pay the debt we owe. The crime will be expunged from our record and placed on His. He bears our sin debt, and we go free with a spotless record.

*2.* **When we are justified, two things take place. We are set free, and our past sins are wiped away. We cannot justify ourselves. Only God is able to do this work in our hearts.**

___ Acts 13:39     a. The law cannot justify anyone in God's sight.

___ Romans 3:20    b. We are justified by faith in Jesus Christ.

___ Romans 3:24    c. We are justified by grace and given hope of eternal life.

___ Romans 4:2     d. We are justified freely by grace through redemption.

___ Galatians 2:16  e. Everyone who believes is justified from all things.

___ Galatians 3:11  f. If we were justified by works, we could boast about it.

___ Titus 3:7      g. The just shall live by faith.

We were not just forgiven from sin, we are freed from our slavery to it! "Do you not know that to whom you present yourselves slaves to obey, you are that one's slaves whom you obey, whether of sin leading to death, or of obedience leading to righteousness?" (Rom. 6:16 NKJV). Before Jesus, we were enslaved by sin and helpless to escape its thrall. Ruled by our own selfish impulses, we lived as enemies of God. Freed from sin's reign, we are able to live ruled by the Spirit. "But now having been set free from sin, and having become slaves of God, you have your fruit to reflect the influence of our new Lord, they prove we haven't only been justified, but we are also being sanctified." (Rom. 6:22)

*3. Sanctification is the process of spiritual cleansing—the purification of our souls on an everyday basis.*

- Who sanctifies us, according to Jude 1?

_____

_____

● What is one of the means of sanctification mentioned in Acts 20:32?

_____

_____

● What is a sanctified person good for, according to 2 Timothy 2:21?

_____

_____

## Did You Know?

*Most of the books of the New Testament are written by apostles—Paul, John, Peter, Matthew. Three of the books were written by disciples who were right there with the apostles—Mark and Luke. But did you realize that a couple of them were written by Jesus' own half-brothers? Joseph and Mary had added to their family over the years after that famous Christmas birth, so Jesus had a passel of little brothers and sisters. James and Jude, who each grew up with Jesus as their big brother, contributed books to our Bible canon.*

Becoming sanctified means setting aside our own selfish desires and fleshly appetites. Instead, we ask the Spirit to come in and have "all of me." When this happens, we begin to see spiritual fruit growing in our lives—love, joy, peace, patience, kindness, goodness, faithfulness, gentleness, and self-control.

*4. There are illustrations in Scripture of God sanctifying things for His purposes, and there are verses that tell us how God goes about sanctifying believers. This list includes both—match them up!*

___ Genesis 2:3

a. We are sanctified by the truth.

___ Exodus 29:43

b. God sanctified people for His service.

___ Numbers 3:13

c. We are sanctified by the Word of God and prayer.

___ Jeremiah 1:5

d. God sanctified the Sabbath day.

___ John 17:19

e. God sanctified all the firstborn in Israel.

___ 1 Corinthians 1:2

f. We are sanctified by God's will, through Christ's sacrifice.

___ 1 Timothy 4:5

g. God sanctified the tabernacle.

___ Hebrews 10:10

h. We are sanctified in Christ Jesus.

Sanctification is an ongoing process in a believer's life. We will never be finished with it in this world. "He who has begun a good work in you will complete it" (Phil. 1:6 NKJV). But that completion cannot happen until our souls are free from the lingering results of sin's presence in the world. That will happen when we are glorified.

*5. Glorification is the final phase of salvation. It is salvation fully realized.*

- After what event did the disciples begin to understand Jesus' fulfillment of the prophecies, according to John 12:16?

● In the progression of events given in Romans 8:30, what does Paul say is our ultimate end?

_____

_____

● Paul says that because we have shared in Christ's suffering, what else will we share with Him, according to Romans 8:17?

_____

_____

When we say that Christians have been given hope, what is that hope? We have said that one hope is the lifting of the curse of sin. Another hope is of seeing Jesus at His Second Coming. But the granddaddy of all hopes—the one that is mentioned most often in the Scriptures—is the hope for eternal life. That is the ultimate hope that was given to us at salvation.

6. *Paul provides us with a very nice summary of salvation in Romans 5:1, 2. Fill in the blanks of his statement here.*

Therefore, having been _____ by _____, we have _____ with _____ through our Lord Jesus Christ, through whom also we have _____ by _____ into this _____ in which we _____, and _____ in _____ of the _____ of God. —Romans 5:1, 2 NKJV

We all have a past—where we came from, where we've been, what we've experienced. We all have the present—responsibilities to see to, choices to make, moments to savor. And we all have a future—the result of today's decisions, the unexpected bend in the road, and an eternal hope. Past, present, future. Yesterday, today, tomorrow. What was, and is, and is to come. I can look back at the girl I once was. I can see what kind of a person I have become. And in every phase of life, I can see

God's hand, justifying and sanctifying. I can also look forward to the kind of woman I hope to be. Then, I will be glorified.

## PRAYING GOD'S PROMISES

Paul's divinely inspired explanations of the intricacies of our faith are clear-sighted, if a bit wordy. Here is a Scripture prayer based on just a few verses—Romans 8:15–18—that are packed full with precious truths.

*Abba, Father, You are my Father. Released from sin's bondage, rescued from fear, chosen, and adopted. Adopted! I'm not one of Your people, not a descendent of Abraham. I'm an outsider, a Gentile. But I have received Your Spirit, and He bears witness in my soul, that I belong to You now. I am Your child. I am an heir in Your household. You have made me a joint-heir with Jesus, and I will receive the same inheritance He did—life. Someday, You will come for me, and I will be glorified. That is the hope that pulls me through the rough days. These little sufferings will be nothing compared with the glory that will be revealed in me. Oh, I ache for that day. It will be glorious! Amen.*

***Now you shall write a prayer.*** Here is another Scripture passage in which our hearts are described as calling out to God as our "Abba, Father"—basically, that's Aramaic for Daddy. Journal your prayer here.

*Even so we, when we were children, were in bondage under the elements of the world. But when the fullness of the time had come, God sent forth His Son, born of a woman, born under the law, to redeem those who were under the law, that we might receive the adoption as sons. And because you are sons, God has sent forth the Spirit of His Son into your hearts, crying out, "Abba, Father!" Therefore you are no longer a slave but a son, and if a son, then an heir of God through Christ.*

Galatians 4:3–7 NKJV

## DAY THREE

# HOW LONG, LORD!

*"We through the Spirit eagerly wait for the hope
of righteousness by faith."*
Galatians 5:5 NKJV

The ninth month. Although there are many small inconveniences and discomforts for an expectant mother throughout the three trimesters of pregnancy, nothing compares with the ninth month. These last few weeks are when all the little things begin to pile up—fatigue, swelling, leg cramps, strange cravings, muscle spasms, aching in the lower back, and frequent, urgent trips to the bathroom. As our hormones rage, we have a tendency to dissolve into tears on a moment's notice. There's a decided waddle to our walk, and it becomes impossible to find a comfortable sleeping position. Well-intentioned people state the obvious, "My, you are getting big!" or the doubtful, "You've never looked more beautiful." Our belly button pops inside out. Our bra size goes up by three cups. The taut skin stretched across our abdomen itches. Our legs become restless, and tiny contractions start up but go nowhere. Each of these things, alone, would be easy to take in stride, but put altogether, they become a heavy load to bear. So whenever people ask a friendly, "How are you doing?" The answer we all give is, "I just want to get this over with." We begin to look forward, with more and more fervency and urgency, to delivery. The first thought in our head when we wake each morning is, "I wonder if it will be today?" The first thought in our head as we try to settle down for the night is, "I wonder if it will be tonight." Every particle of our being, every fiber of our body is consciously and subconsciously tensed for that first twinge. We know it is coming. We just don't know when.

This is the very kind of expectancy that we should have regarding the return of Jesus. Whether consciously or unconsciously, we are tensed for the sound of the trumpet's blast. We're eager. We're impatient. We're watchful. The first thought we have each morning is, "Today?" and the first thought we have as we go to bed for the night is, "Tonight?" We know Jesus is coming. We just don't know when.

*1.* *Waiting is hard, especially when we don't know when the end of waiting might come. Enduring is easier if we know when it will be over. It is much harder to be patient when no end is in sight. Over and over and over in the psalms, David would ask God, "How long?" What was he watching for in Psalm 90:13?*

_____

_____

_____

_____

_____

_____

_____

_____

_____

How much longer? We don't know. We won't know. "The Son of Man is coming at an hour you do not expect." (Matt. 24:44 NKJV). Do you like surprises? Because the return of Jesus will be one! All we can do is be ready, and look for it.

*2.* *There are times when we are like children, impatient through the duration of a car ride. We repeatedly ask, "How much longer?" and "Are we there yet?" When was David impatient for God to act? Match up these examples.*

___ Psalm 6:3        a. How long will you let the enemy insult
                          Your name?

___ Psalm 13:1       b. How long will You hide from me?

___ Psalm 35:17      c. How long will wicked people triumph?

___ Psalm 74:10    d. How long must I feel as if You've forgotten me?

___ Psalm 79:5     e. How long must I remain troubled?

___ Psalm 89:46    f. How long will You be angry with me?

___ Psalm 94:3     g. How long before You come to my rescue?

When the time came for Jesus to return to His Father in heaven, He reassured His disciples. "I have to go away now. If I don't go, I won't be able to come back!" Every generation of believers since theirs has been hoping that they would be the one to see Christ's return. Perhaps it will be ours!

*3. To Jesus' way of thinking, how long would it be before His return, according to John 16:19?*

_____

_____

_____

_____

_____

_____

Have you ever had to deal with someone who has no real concept of time? They make unrealistic plans for their day, neglecting to figure in preparation time, travel time, and downtime. Their concept of punctuality might be tactfully called relaxed. They're the kind of people who are always running behind with their work, always the last to arrive, always late. What's more, they are blissfully unaware of the havoc they reek with other people's schedules. (They think we're too uptight!) I've often wondered if Jesus needed a firmer grasp on the concept of time. If He was to return in "a little while," He seems to be running a bit late!

**4.** *Believe it or not, everything is right on schedule. Why does 2 Peter 3:9 say that God has "delayed" Jesus' return?*

_____

_____

_____

_____

_____

_____

_____

_____

So here is another area in which we need to just sit back and trust God. Our hope is coming. Nothing can keep it back. But the Father, out of love and mercy, has delayed it for a bit. He's giving as many people as possible the chance to find eternal life through Christ. He's delaying so that we have just a little more time to get the Good News out!

**5.** *Meanwhile, we wait eagerly. We can't help it. "How long, Lord," is still the cry of our hearts.*

Romans 8:23—Even we ourselves _____ within _____, eagerly _____ for the _____, the _____ of our _____.

Romans 8:25—If we _____ for what we do not _____, we _____ for it with _____.

1 Corinthians 1:7— . . . _____ _____ for the _____ of our Lord Jesus Christ.

> The Lord isn't really being slow about his promise to return, as some people think. No, he is being patient for your sake. He does not want anyone to perish, so he is giving more time for everyone to repent.
>
> 2 Peter 3:9 NLT

Galatians 5:5—We through the Spirit _____ _____ for the _____ of _____ by _____ .

Philippians 3:20—Our _____ is in _____ , from which we also _____ _____ for the _____ , the Lord Jesus Christ.

Hebrews 9:28—To those who _____ _____ for Him He will _____ a _____ _____ , apart from sin, for _____ .

Jesus' return is inevitable. His coming is imminent. He might be just one more day, one more hour, one more minute, one more moment from being revealed. The time could be now. This could be the day. Or as my mother used to say when we'd pester her about suppertime, "It'll be ready when your father gets home, and he'll be here when he gets here."

*6. What was Peter looking for, according to 2 Peter 3:12?*

_____

_____

_____

_____

_____

_____

_____

_____

*7. What stance did Paul say we should take, while we are waiting, according to 1 Corinthians 16:13?*

_____

_____

Literature is filled with characters who rise above their desperate circumstances, do the impossible, and triumph in the end. Take Cinderella. She was forced to set aside her rights as a daughter and take on the rags of a slave. Though she endured constant persecution, she retained her sweet nature. And in the end, when jealousy, hatred, and deception failed to hide her loveliness from the Prince, she was carried off to live happily ever after. Nowadays, all kinds of come-from-behind situations are compared with hers. Teams from small schools that make it to the play-offs are called Cinderella teams. People who have gone from rags to riches are said to have Cinderella stories.

We, too, are waiting for our Prince to come. How long will it be until He arrives? As long as it takes. Only God knows. So we will have the pleasure of a surprise. It is enough to know that He is coming, and we will join Him then.

## PRAYING GOD'S PROMISES

Today's prayer will be based on one of David's "How long, Lord?" psalms—Psalm 90:12–17.

*Long-awaited Savior, How long will it be before Your return? It could be at any moment, so teach me to number my days. I'm thankful for Your mercy, which allows more men and women to find eternal life. While I am waiting, teach me to rejoice and be glad for each new day. Show me Your mighty works. Be glorified in my life. Let the beauty of Your presence be seen in me. Give me a heart of wisdom. Teach me how precious each day is. Establish the work of my hands. May my efforts for Your sake be good and useful and sure. Amen.*

*You should live holy lives and serve God, as you wait for and look forward to the coming of the day of God. When that day comes, the skies will be destroyed with fire, and everything in them will melt with heat. But God made a promise to us, and we are waiting for a new heaven and a new earth where goodness lives. Dear friends, since you are waiting for this to happen, do your best to be without sin and without fault. Try to be at peace with God. Remember that we are saved because our Lord is patient.*

2 Peter 3:11–15 NCV

For your journaled prayer, take 2 Peter 3:11–15 as your inspiration. In it, Peter describes some of the things we should be about, while we are waiting.

## DAY FOUR

# FACE-TO-FACE

*"They shall see His face."*
Revelation 22:4 NKJV

We live in a day and age that provides us with dozens of ways to communicate with one another. Telephones, answering machines, fax machines, pagers, cellular phones, voice mail, e-mail, snail mail, and instant messaging. So many people have cell phones now, you can't sit through a meeting without someone's purse or pocket ringing. We act like children with a new set of walkie-talkies! However, none of these marvels of modern technology can replace a good face-to-face chat. Some news is best shared in person. Some confidences are best traded in a whisper. Some statements are best delivered point blank. Why? Because words on a page and letters on a screen cannot convey all the nuances of facial expressions, even if you do use smilies! :-) How can you gauge a first reaction if you are not there to witness it? There is as much meaning to be drawn from the facial expression and body language of the person you're talking to as might be found in their actual words. The set of the mouth, the furrowing of the brow, the flush of embarrassment, the shiftiness of dishonesty, the twinkle of humor, a flash of anger, stiffness in the posture, a look of patent boredom, a sarcastic inflection, a hint of uncertainty, a wink, a fading smile, a disappointed pout, the verge of tears, a roll of the eyes, a frown of confusion, a shrug of the shoulders, the tapping of a toe, a curled lip, the shine of delight, a gasp of surprise, the look of love.

As Christians living in the twenty-first century, we have never seen Jesus face to face. We've never looked into His eyes. We don't know what His smile looks like. But, oh, how we want to see His precious face, and to look into His eyes and find love there.

*1. Hope gives us something to look forward to. In a way, hope gives us a unique perspective on things, because we see things that the rest of the world is still blind to.*

- How does Paul describe the things believers are aware of in 2 Corinthians 4:18?

- What did Stephen see when the heavens opened up to him in Acts 7:56?

- And what does Peter say we need to be looking for, according to 2 Peter 3:13?

*2.* **What does John, the beloved disciple, tell us is in store, according to 1 John 3:2?**

_____

_____

_____

_____

_____

_____

_____

## Did You Know?

The two books that Paul wrote to the Thessalonian church were sent to comfort and encourage the believers there. They'd become the victims of some false teachers, and they were very confused. One of the reasons that 1 and 2 Thessalonians are our best sources of information about the return of Jesus is that the people in Thessalonica thought that they had missed the Second Coming, and they were panicking over their dilemma. Paul wrote to assure them that they hadn't been left behind, and certain things would have to happen before Jesus would return.

*3.* **Paul must have chuckled to himself when he heard that the Thessalonian church thought they had missed Jesus' return. There will be no mistaking the Second Coming of Jesus.**

● When Jesus comes again, who will see it, according to Luke 3:6?

_____

_____

● What prophecy will be fulfilled at that time, according to Romans 14:11?

_____

_____

● When the Bible says every, who all is included, according to Philippians 2:10, 11?

_____

_____

God didn't tell us every detail of His plans. We don't need to know everything, so long as we trust Him. But our Bibles contain all the information we need for salvation. And Jesus provides everything we need for life and godly living (2 Pet. 1:3).

4. **How does Paul describe our understanding of spiritual things? Fill in the blanks.**

When that which is _____ has come, then
that which is _____ _____ will be
_____ _____. . .For
_____ we _____ in
a _____, _____, but
then _____ to _____.
Now I _____ in _____,
but then I shall _____ just as I also am
_____. —1 Cor. 13:10, 12 NKJV

Everything that we know about God now has been revealed to us in His Word, and yet this certainly does not encompass all that He is. We are given a glimpse of His glory. We only see in part. But when we reach glory, the perfect will replace our partial understanding. We shall see our Savior face-to-face. We will grasp things our minds could not hold now. And we will know the Lord just as He knows us.

*5. What will happen when believers finally meet Jesus, according to Revelation 22:4?*

_____

_____

_____

_____

_____

_____

_____

_____

_____

_____

Can you imagine it? We will meet the Man who sacrificed everything for us. We'll stand in the presence of the One who created the universe. We'll look into the eyes of the One who made us uniquely us. We'll see those famous scars. We'll hear His voice. We'll be able to say thank You. We'll be able to worship at His feet. And that will be just the beginning of forever! What a glorious hope we cherish!

*6. What will Jesus give to each of us when we arrive in glory, according to Revelation 2:17?*

_____

_____

_____

_____

_____

We will be cherished. We will finally understand. We will be face-to-face with Jesus. Everything will be beyond our wildest dreams. It will take our breath away. We will be deliriously, wondrously, gloriously joyful. Everything will be perfect. We'll be able to serve God without stumbling. We'll be able to worship Him right up close. The very thought of it makes our souls tremble with eagerness.

## Praying God's Promises

Others have longed to see God's face. Moses begged the Lord to show His glorious presence to him. This prayer is based on that conversation between Moses and God, found in Exodus 33:18–23.

*Glorious Lord, I long to see Your face. I'm like Moses, begging again and again for the chance to see You. You showed kindness and mercy to him when You hid him in the cleft of the rock and passed by. All of Your goodness passed before Moses, and You spoke Your name in His presence. You couldn't let him see Your face. It would have been too much for any man to stand. Even though all he was permitted to see was Your retreating back, Moses was changed by his encounter with You. For days, his face glowed. I want to live in Your presence. I want to see Your face. And I want to be so changed by my encounters with You that Your presence leaves a glow. Someday, I will see Your face! I will never be the same. Amen.*

**Now it is your turn.** Do you remember the beatitude that says, "Blessed are the peacemakers for they shall see God"? Well, today, you can go through all the Beatitudes and formulate your prayer from their promises.

*You're blessed when you're at the end of your rope. With less of you there is more of God and his rule. You're blessed when you feel you've lost what is most dear to you. Only then can you be embraced by the One most dear to you. You're blessed when you're content with just who you are—no more, no less. That's the moment you find yourselves proud owners of everything that can't be bought. You're blessed when you've worked up a good appetite for God. He's food and drink in the best meal you'll ever eat. You're blessed when you care. At the moment of being "carefull," you find yourselves cared for. You're blessed when you get your inside world—your mind and heart—put right. Then you can see God in the outside world. You're blessed when you can show people how to cooperate instead of compete or fight. That's when you discover who you really are, and your place in God's family.*

Matthew 5:3–9 MSG

## DAY FIVE

# DEATH HAS NO STING

*"O Death, where is your sting? O Hades, where is your victory?"*
1 Corinthians 15:55 NKJV

My youngest has never liked the church nursery. As soon as he was old enough to know what was going on around him, he developed separation anxiety. It's difficult to assure a little person that you will be returning very soon. The time apart will be over quickly, and then you'll come back to pick him up. All he knew was that Daddy and Mama were leaving him behind. By the time he was a year old, just pulling into the church parking lot would turn his normally cheerful disposition strangely quiet. When we'd reach the hallway to the nursery, he'd start to whimper. Once he was walking, he'd dig in his heels and try to pull away. As we'd sign him in and turn him over to the waiting attendants, sorrow and mourning had taken over his little face. Tears rolling freely down his cheeks, he would weep copiously, clinging tightly to the nursery worker for comfort. He never got angry. He never kicked and screamed. He was just sad. The nursery ladies always smiled to see him coming, happy to cuddle and comfort him, and murmuring things like, "Bless his heart."

As believers, I think we face death the same way. We might grow quiet and drag our feet just a little. But we don't kick and scream against it. We know that when we're parted from someone we love dearly, that it will only be for a short time. Separation makes us sad. But there is no sting of despair. We have no need to fear death. Jesus robbed it of its power over us.

*1.* **How did Paul describe the victory of Jesus over sin and death in 1 Corinthians 15:54? Fill in the blanks.**

So when this _____ (that means our sin-corrupted bodies)

Has put on _____ (that means being given a new, glorified body)

and this _____ (that means something temporary, that can die)

has put on _____ (that means living forever!)

then shall be _____ to _____ (that means a fulfillment of prophecy)

the saying that is written: "_____ is _____ up (all gone!)

in _____." (that means Jesus wins!)

*2.* **These words are quoted so often at funerals, they are familiar to believers and nonbelievers alike. What does David say comforts him in the face of death in Psalm 23:4?**

## Did You Know?

*The ancient shepherds had two basic tools of the trade—a rod and a staff. The staff was the familiar shepherd's crook, used as a walking stick throughout the day's journey. With it, a shepherd could tap the sheep into line, keeping the herd together and directing them along safe paths. The hooked end of the staff could be used to rescue a sheep that had fallen into a crevice. The rod was a kind of club or cudgel, which was used to drive away predators. It served to protect the flock.*

David knew the life of a shepherd so well—he'd been raised to it. The watchful eye, the gentle correction, the protection from enemies, the wise guidance—David had come to depend upon them just as sheep depend upon their shepherd. He trusted God completely to lead him, even through "the valley of the shadow of death"—life-threatening circumstances and life-and-death decisions.

*3.* **What does Hebrews 2:15 say that we are released from?**

Death holds no sting for the believer. Even in these days when there are terrorist scares, random bombings, strange new diseases, and equally deadly old ones. We need not fear them. Neither should we worry about those who might try to harm us. Jesus said, "Don't be afraid of those who want to kill you. They can only kill your body; they cannot touch your soul" (Matt. 10:28 NLT). Even in the face of death, we are kept safe. The eternal part of us can never be touched by an enemy.

*4. Paul lays out the logistics of life and death quite neatly in 2 Corinthians 5:6–9.*

- What does it mean if we are at home in the body, according to verse 6?

- What does it mean if we are absent from the body, according to verse 8?

- Which of these two options pleases Paul more?

- With all that in mind, what is Paul's aim, according to verse 9?

The image is a familiar one, made commonplace by television and movies. A group of mourners, huddled under umbrellas at a graveside service. Everyone is draped in black—suits and coats and veiled hats. Women weep softly into their handkerchiefs, and men clench their jaws and keep their eyes downcast. Every face registers shock and despair and regret. The blankness of despair dims every eye. But this is not the grieving of believers.

*5. Our hearts do grieve at the loss of a loved one, but the Bible assures us that there is hope.*

- What hope is recorded in Acts 24:15?

_____

_____

- What does Paul remind us about in 1 Thessalonians 4:13, 14?

_____

_____

Christians who have died are not lost to us forever. They are merely asleep in Jesus. When Jesus comes for us, He will return for them as well! The hope we hold so dearly includes the hope of seeing our loved ones again. What's more, we are going to be rid of death once and for all.

*6. Heaven holds the promise of change. Things won't be the same as we have known them all our lives. Change might be scary at times, but you'll have to agree that these all sound like changes for the better! Fill in these blanks, based on Revelation 21:4.*

No more _____

No more _____

No more _____

No more _____

## PRAYING GOD'S PROMISES

First Corinthians 15:51–57 has a familiar feel to it, especially if you enjoy listening to Handel's "Messiah" during the holidays each year.

These verses provide the text for one of its songs. Today, it will serve as the basis for our Scripture prayer.

*Living God, You have revealed great mysteries to Your people. A time is coming soon when we shall all be changed. A trumpet will sound, and in the twinkling of an eye, our lives will be something new. The dead will be raised. Our new forms will be incorruptible—eternal. We will have victory over death. Death's sting will be removed. And all because of Jesus. Thank You, God, for telling us this ahead of time. I do not fear death. I look forward to Jesus' call. Amen.*

For your Scripture prayer today, take Romans 6:9–14 as your foundation. In it, Paul declares Jesus' triumph over death—it has no dominion over Him! See if you can't transform it into a prayer of praise.

> *Christ, having been raised from the dead, dies no more. Death no longer has dominion over Him. For the death that He died, He died to sin once for all; but the life that He lives, He lives to God. Likewise you also, reckon yourselves to be dead indeed to sin, but alive to God in Christ Jesus our Lord. Therefore do not let sin reign in your mortal body, that you should obey it in its lusts. And do not present your members as instruments of unrighteousness to sin, but present yourselves to God as being alive from the dead, and your members as instruments of righteousness to God. For sin shall not have dominion over you, for you are not under law but under grace.*
>
> Romans 6:9–14 NKJV

## CONCLUSION

It isn't any wonder at all that the early Christians were willing to suffer and die for the hope they had in Jesus. No one would trade passing fancies for eternal treasures. What does it matter if people frustrate, embarrass, persecute, or kill us? They cannot touch our eternal souls. When we see our hopes fulfilled, we will have life—new life, sinless life, holy life, glorified life, eternal life. We will be with Jesus. And Paul promises that it will be better than anything we could ever imagine. Hope leaves death without any sting. And hope is worth living for. We must hope until the end.

### JOURNALING SUGGESTIONS

Once you are glorified—having received a new body and been rid of your sin nature—what will remain? What facets of your personality will remain firmly, uniquely you?

If you knew you were going to be whisked away for a long journey on a moment's notice, who would you want to speak with before you left and what would your last words to them be?

Good friends, couples, and parents have mastered certain forms of face-to-face, nonverbal communication. No words are needed. Just a look or a gesture. What are you able to communicate to those close to you without uttering a single word?

Jesus' return will have an element of surprise to it. Have you ever planned a surprise party for someone? Why do you suppose we get so much pleasure out of these events?

Have you ever stopped to consider who you are most looking forward to seeing when you get to heaven? We all want to see Jesus, but what about friends, family, or heroes of the faith? Who do you want to talk to?

### JOURNALING QUOTE

*Some of you have been journaling for years, and it is as comfortable to you as your slippers in the evening. But for others this will be a new process. Relax. Keeping a journal should never be a pressure; it is an invitation to an oasis, like quiet time with God.*

Nicole Johnson

# LESSON 6

# HOPE UNTIL THE END

*"Christ as a Son over His own house, whose house we are
if we hold fast the confidence and the rejoicing of the hope firm to the end."*
Hebrews 3:6 NKJV

## INTRODUCTION BY NICOLE JOHNSON

Do you ever find in the course of your day that you can't do certain things because they are connected to other things that haven't been done yet? You need to make travel plans, but the dates of the trip haven't been finalized yet. You have four packages to take to the post office right away, but you are still waiting on the correct address for one more letter. You've decided to recover chairs in your living room, but you can't pick the fabric and start the process because you haven't found the exact sofa you're looking for.

Much of life is lived trying to work together the pieces of the known and the unknown. We can recognize certain shapes and patterns, but we don't always know where they fit, or what they mean. Sometimes my life feels like a giant puzzle that I can't figure out. Everything is connected, but how do all the pieces fit together, and how can I keep going when I can't see what the end result is supposed to be? How can I keep from being discouraged by the bigness of life or being overwhelmed by the dailyness of all the little things?

It might be helpful to try to see this jumble of pieces like a puzzle that we might work on our kitchen table. First, let's put on some coffee. Then, if you're like me, you go right for the straight edges to try to frame the big picture, which helps me know where certain things go. There are strong truths that we can know for sure, and we can choose those truths to form the framework of our lives. We don't have to have every piece, but we must have enough to find some structure. We can trust God's love for us, put our faith in Him, and acknowledge the biblical straight edges that He provides for our lives. Unfortunately, there is no real box top to look at for the big picture, so we just start to look for the colors of love and kindness, patience and goodness, and put them in place accordingly. We soon find that pieces that don't seem to fit together often do, like suffering and joy, and then we see something in the picture we didn't see before.

When you work a puzzle, you have to constantly adjust your vision to see the big picture and the little pieces at the same time. Every once in a while, when you get lost in the pieces, you have to pull back and look at the work you've done, such as in the right-hand corner section of the puzzle. Only then can you see how everything has worked together for the good of your overall picture. This kind of understanding of life helps me keep going. I can trust that there are more pieces that are going to fall into place, and I also recognize that there are holes that I can't fill just yet. So when I feel overwhelmed and I can't find the pieces I'm looking for, or when nothing seems to fit, I go to the straight edges and concentrate again on those. I try to remember the simple truths, and they help me to get my bearings. I remember that to keep my hope until the end, I must hold the big picture and the little pieces at the same time. So I put on another pot of coffee and keep going.

Hope is real. It's bright. It's sure. All that's left is the waiting for its fulfillment. We know that someday our Prince will come back—we just don't know when. The uncertainty of the time frame and long centuries of silence have dulled our sense of anticipation. There are so many other things to take care of that thoughts of a soon-coming King get pushed to the back burner. Far too easily, we're lulled into a sense of complacency. Instead of facing each morning with an eager, "Maybe today!" we shrug our shoulders and say, "Why should it be today? It's no more special than any other day." Hope is out of sight, and out of mind. But that's not the way we're supposed to live. Over and over, Jesus says, "Watch!" The disciples urge us to be prepared, be ready, and be busy about the Lord's business. This last week, we'll talk about keeping hope fresh in our heart, maintaining a sense of eagerness and urgency about the Lord's return, and continuing to serve God faithfully. In this way, we will hang on to hope right up until the end.

### A Peek at Our Week:

- **Day One:** Strengthening Hope
- **Day Two:** Boldness to Proclaim
- **Day Three:** While There Is Life, There Is Hope
- **Day Four:** Hopeful Preparations
- **Day Five:** Hope and Wait Quietly

# DAY ONE

## STRENGTHENING HOPE

*"Be of good courage, And He shall strengthen your heart,*
*All you who hope in the LORD."*
Psalm 31:24 NKJV

There's nothing more depressing than a waiting room. There are all kinds of waiting rooms. Doctor's offices and emergency rooms come immediately to mind. But have you ever been inside the waiting rooms at car service stations? (Shudder.) Or do you remember the last time you had to update your driver's license? (Take a number.) Whether you have an appointment or it's a dire emergency, the routine is pretty much the same wherever you go. You walk up to a receptionist, validate your identity, and fill out the necessary forms. Then you are politely pointed to a chair and asked to wait. Waiting rooms are universally unsuited to their purpose. Their atmosphere does little to help you relax. Cold tile floors or industrial strength carpeting designed to withstand heavy foot traffic. Outdated color schemes. Hard plastic chairs. Glaring fluorescent lights. The pervasive odor of disinfectants. Their amenities do nothing to divert our attention. Three-year-old magazines, sickly-looking potted plants, racks of medical brochures, televisions with the sound turned off. All we can do is settle down into our chair and prepare ourselves to endure the wait.

We have a precious hope, and we know that it will be fulfilled someday. All that's left is the waiting. But we're not stranded in some stark waiting room for the duration. We're not gritting our teeth to endure an interminable wait. We're not just putting in our time until the Second Coming. Hope strengthens us for the wait. It motivates us for the work that lies ahead.

*1. There are times when we have to ask ourselves, "What's the problem here?" David asked himself that question more than once. Psalm 42:5; 42:11; and 43:5 all ask the same question.*

*Why are you cast down, O my soul? And why are you disquieted within me?* (NKJV)

*Why am I discouraged? Why so sad?* (NLT)

*Why am I so sad? Why am I so upset?* (NCV)

*Why are you down in the dumps, dear soul? Why are you crying the blues?* (MSG)

What was David's answer each time?

_____

_____

_____

_____

_____

_____

_____

_____

_____

_____

_____

One of the hardest things to be strong through are times when we just don't feel like it. There's no use denying that times of weariness, depression, and sadness come. They do. Even David knew that. But even when we're singing the blues, we can do just what David did in his psalms. Redirect our thoughts heavenward. Remind ourselves about the hope that is ours. Fix our eyes on God, and ask Him to strengthen us through the low days.

*2. God is our strength, and we count on Him for the umph we need on a day-to-day basis. Take a look at these different verses that promise strength to the hope-filled heart. Match them up!*

___ Psalm 27:14    a. God's hand establishes us. His arm strengthens us.

___ Psalm 68:28    b. The God of all grace will strengthen you.

___ Psalm 89:21    c. Wait on the Lord, and He will strengthen your heart.

___ Isaiah 41:10    d. Don't be afraid. God will strengthen and help us.

___ 1 Peter 5:10    e. God has commanded your strength.

Rough days. Tough days. Restless days. Cranky days. Melancholy days. Weepy days. Lackluster days. Stressful days. Reminiscent days. Grouchy days. Snappish days. Shouting days. Blah days. Meager days. Fearful days. Bleak days. Gloomy days. Bland days. Worried days. Average days. These are the times when we need hope's strength.

*3. We are strong when we are sure. What assurances do the Scriptures give us?*

• What is Solomon sure of in Proverbs 23:18?

_____

_____

• What does God assure us in Jeremiah 29:11?

_____

_____

A hope and a future. What a comforting promise. The Hebrew word that is translated hope here would be best translated "expected." So a more literal reading of Jeremiah 29:11 would be, "to give you an end that is expected," or "to give you an expected future." For the Old Testament Jews, they were awaiting the end of their captivity to the Babylonians.

For believers now, we are awaiting the end of our captivity to sin. Jesus is our hope. He is our expected future.

*4. We talk a lot about character building.*

- What builds character, according to Romans 5:4?

  _____

  _____

- What does character strengthen, according to Romans 5:4?

  _____

  _____

- What does a strong character make you ready for, according to James 1:4?

  _____

  _____

> *And endurance develops strength of character in us, and character strengthens our confident expectation of salvation.*
>
> Romans 5:4 NLT

Hope keeps us focused. It's like the compass needle, pointing to true north. It keeps us plodding on the straight and narrow path. It guides us unerringly in the right direction. Hope points us toward our end goal, the finish line, our prize. It reminds us of our incentive. It leads us true. With hope in our hearts, we keep on living to please our Lord, knowing that it will all be worth it in the end.

*5. Keep your focus. Stay strong. Hang in there. Keep hoping. Take a look at Hebrews 6:11 in its various translations. Underline the description of our effort found in each.*

- We desire that each one of you show the same diligence to the full assurance of hope until the end (NKJV).

  _____

  _____

- We want each of you to go on with the same hard work all your lives so you will surely get what you hope for (NCV).

- Our great desire is that you will keep right on loving others as long as life lasts, in order to make certain that what you hope for will come true (NLT).

- I want each of you to extend that same intensity toward a full-bodied hope, and keep at it till the finish (MSG).

Hebrews characterizes us as diligent, hard-working, intense people. We aren't just drifting along, letting the current carry us to an eventual end. We are working toward that hope—paddling steadily all the way.

*6. Hope is ours. We are assured of its promise. So what is our attitude while we wait? What does wise Solomon say in Ecclesiastes 5:20?*

*But may the God of all grace, who called us to His eternal glory by Christ Jesus, after you have suffered a while, perfect, establish, strengthen, and settle you.*

1 Peter 5:10 NKJV

*You also be patient. Establish your hearts, for the coming of the Lord is at hand.*

James 5:8 NKJV

*Now may our Lord Jesus Christ Himself, and our God and Father, who has loved us and given us everlasting consolation and good hope by grace, comfort your hearts and establish you in every good word and work.*

2 Thessalonians 2:16, 17 NKJV

The fact that we are waiting women doesn't prevent us from being used by God. Hope doesn't cause us to pine away into listless longing. We aren't so distracted by our expectation that we become too heavenly-minded to do any earthly good. Quite the contrary. Hope motivates us for the task at hand. It gives us courage for the wait ahead. Hope strengthens us.

### PRAYING GOD'S PROMISES

God alone can give us strength. He alone is able to establish us. Today's prayer is based on Paul's closing prayer in the Book of Romans—Romans 16:25–27. Among other things, he asks God to establish us through Jesus.

*Source of Strength, You alone are able to establish me. You are my only source of strength. You are my only source of salvation. Thank You for sending Jesus with His words of life. Thank You for revealing Your secret plan of salvation. You are so wise! I'm so thankful to have heard it and believed. Lord, let more people know. Let all the nations hear. You are the everlasting God, and You deserve glory from all people. May the followers of Jesus give You greater glory as each day passes. Amen.*

***Now it is your turn.*** Consider the three verses printed in the margin here, and use them as the inspiration for your own prayer today.

# DAY TWO

## BOLDNESS TO PROCLAIM

*"Therefore, since we have such hope,*
*we use great boldness of speech."*

2 Corinthians 3:12 NKJV

There are plenty of things that you can be completely sure about. You've got your facts straight, you've been briefed, you're in the loop. Red means stop and green means go. Fires are hot. Ice is cold. Moldy food is best left untasted. Ask yourself what kinds of things can you "know in your knower" with certainty. Are you absolutely, positively sure whether you are right- or left-handed? (Of course!) Do you know, beyond a shadow of a doubt, how to tie your shoes? (Years of experience!) Can you, without a question in your mind, state your own middle name? (Yes, yes, yes.) These examples might seem a little absurd. We know these things because they are a part of us. They are the "givens" in our lives—so basic, so automatic. We know them from long experience. We can do them without even thinking. We can't imagine things being any other way. The way we wash our hair. The way we pull up our panty hose. The way we brush our teeth. Simple, repetitious chores—typing, knitting, braiding, kneading—our hands get the feel for them. Sometimes we say that these things have become second nature.

Do you know God well? Are you so familiar with the pages of your Bible that you could say you know it like the back of your hand? Are the truths of Scripture so ingrained in your heart that they have become second nature? Do you accept His commands and promises with the same assurance you have that gravity works and time goes on? The reason a Christian can walk boldly in faith and speak boldly about her faith is this—she knows it.

*1. Some truths are foundational to our faith. We couldn't be called believers without them.*

● What does Deuteronomy 4:39 say that we know in our hearts?

_____

_____

● What do we know about God from Ecclesiastes 3:14?

_____

_____

● What truth do all Christians hold, as we find it in John 6:69?

_____

_____

Do you trust God unreservedly? No niggling doubts. No reservations. No looking back. Your whole life is in His hands. All your eggs are in one basket. You're staunch, you're secure, you're solid. You betcha! It's definite. You're decided. Your faith is firm, fixed, and tied fast. It's a sealed deal. You're confident, convinced, and constant. Unequivocally, unfailingly, unshakably sure. Incontestable, incontrovertible, indisputable. Indubitably!

*2. Facts. Realities. Certainties. Truths. Whatever you want to call them, the Bible is full of them. Here are just a few.*

| | |
|---|---|
| ___ Deuteronomy 4:35 | a. The Holy Spirit dwells in believers. |
| ___ Deuteronomy 7:9 | b. God will be exalted in all the earth. |
| ___ Psalm 46:10 | c. God made us, and we are His people. |
| ___ Psalm 100:3 | d. God is faithful to those who love and obey Him. |
| ___ John 17:3 | e. Believers can know spiritual things. |

___ 1 Corinthians 2:14    f. The Lord is God. There is none beside Him.

___ 1 Corinthians 3:16    g. Knowing God and Jesus brings us eternal life.

We base our morals and decisions on the foundational truths of Scripture. It is the truth, and we trust it completely. From the world's point of view, we are truly a peculiar people. It seemed odd enough to call something as intangible as hope the very anchor of our existence. Now we are living out of a faith that they would call foolish.

*3.* **So what are a people who know God capable of? Fill in the blanks to find out!**

Jeremiah 24:7—I will give them a _____ to _____ Me, that I am the_____; and they shall be _____ _____, and I will be their _____, for they shall _____ to Me with their _____ _____.

Daniel 11:32—The people who _____ their God shall be _____, and carry out _____ _____.

Romans 8:28—We know that all things _____ _____ for _____ to those who _____, to those who are the _____ according to His _____.

1 Corinthians 2:12—Now we have received. . .the _____ who is from _____, that we might _____ the things that have been _____ _____ to us by _____.

*4.* **Knowing the foundations of our faith strengthens our hope. How well do you need to know it, according to 1 Peter 3:15?**

A teacher once told me that I would be sure I understood my material if I could teach it to someone else. In order to explain something to a friend, we need to do some preparation. Going over the facts, thinking through our explanation, putting our thoughts into words—it takes time and effort. When Peter says to be ready to defend our faith, this is what he means. If you are firm in your faith, how would you explain it to someone else in a confident and convincing way?

5. *The very thought of sharing our faith with an unbeliever sets many of us to trembling. But it's no harder to tell people about Jesus now than it was in the days of the apostles. They prayed for boldness, and God provided it. Here are just a few examples. Match them up!*

___ Psalm 138:3      a. The righteous are bold as a lion.

___ Proverbs 28:1      b. We have boldness through faith in Jesus.

___ 2 Corinthians 3:12      c. You made me bold with strength in my soul.

___ Ephesians 3:12      d. Those who serve well obtain great boldness.

___ 1 Timothy 3:13      e. Hope gives us great boldness of speech.

Christianity is not some exclusive hang-out with a "members only" policy. We're not the initiates of some secret club, hiding our rites and rituals from prying eyes. The fellowship of believers does not have a fixed membership, with limited openings available at rare intervals. How silly! Jesus told us from the beginning to get out there and tell as many people as we could about Him. The Lord doesn't want anyone to live ignorant of the way of salvation. So we are to boldly go and tell others what we know so well. When the New Testament says that we should speak with boldness, it means, "without any fear or shame."

*6.* **Take a look at these prayers for boldness throughout the New Testament.**

- What did Peter and John pray for in Acts 4:29?

_____

_____

- How did God answer them in Acts 4:31?

_____

_____

- What did Paul ask people to pray on his behalf in Ephesians 6:19, 20?

_____

_____

We are convinced of the sureness of hope. We know the truth beyond a shadow of a doubt. We are living for the Lord while we await His return. Our boldness in telling others about the Good News is the natural overflow of these things. As the children's song states, "Hide it under a bushel? No! I'm going to let it shine!" Why not make sure as many people as possible share your hope!

## PRAYING GOD'S PROMISES

God's promises are sure, so we can act on them with boldness. Today's prayer is based on a series of verses that tell us that we can live boldly—Philippians 1:20; 1 Thessalonians 2:2; Hebrews 4:16; 10:19; 13:6.

*Knowable God, You give me boldness. Because You are my helper, I have nothing to fear. What can anyone do to me when You hold me secure. You have let me know You through Jesus. Because of His sacrifice, I can enter the Holiest place with boldness. I am welcomed before the very throne of Your grace, and counted as a daughter in Your household. Thank You for hearing me and granting me Your own mercy and grace whenever I have needed it. I am sure of Your greatness and Your power. I have entrusted my life to Your keeping. Give me boldness to speak of You to others. Let my sureness give confidence to my testimony. Amen.*

We know God because He has told us about Himself. When we commit ourselves to faith in His Word, we are changed. For your journaled prayer today, use 1 John 5:18–20 as your foundation. Note how often these verses say, "We know."

*We know that none of the God-begotten makes a practice of sin—fatal sin. The God-begotten are also the God-protected. The Evil One can't lay a hand on them. We know that we are held firm by God; it's only the people of the world who continue in the grip of the Evil One. And we know that the Son of God came so we could recognize and understand the truth of God—what a gift!—and we are living in the Truth itself, in God's Son, Jesus Christ. This Jesus is both True God and Real Life.*

1 John 5:18–20 MSG

## DAY THREE

# WHILE THERE IS LIFE, THERE IS HOPE

*"For him who is joined to all the living there is hope,
for a living dog is better than a dead lion."*
Ecclesiastes 9:4 NKJV

When we lived out in the country, surrounded by cow pastures and cornfields, I kept chickens. We converted a small shed into a coop, installing roosts and nesting boxes. The first shipment of chicks was ordered from Murray McMurray, and our peepers came by mail from Iowa. Since I wanted them mainly for the eggs they would lay, I only ordered hens. Imagine my surprise when early one mid-summer morning, one of my hens developed a peculiar cough. It was a sound that can only be croaked out by an adolescent rooster who is learning to crow. We named him Casanova, and he ruled supreme over his harem of twenty-four hens. But one day, the following spring, tragedy struck. While we were at church on a Sunday morning, a strange dog got into our yard. By the time we returned home, it was too late. Only six hens remained. After cleaning up the mess and shedding a few tears, an idea edged its way into the back of my mind. All hope was not lost. We gathered up all the eggs from the nests in the coop and made a quick call to Murray McMurray. In just a few days, the incubator arrived, and we set it up in the corner of our family room. There was room for forty-eight eggs. In the midst of the shock and despair of losing most of my clucking, pecking, scratching pets, we received an unexpected blessing. Our whole family enjoyed the next three weeks of anticipation. We watched the miracle of life as each egg hatched, adding a new member to our little flock.

Many of us are holding on to the hope that someone dear to our hearts will turn to the Lord before it is too late. All we can see is the pain, the desperation, the sadness, and the hopelessness. We see the mess their lives are in, and we've shed plenty of tears. But God has a surprising way of bringing unexpected blessings. While there is still life, there is still hope. So keep praying!

*1. God loves. Over and over we see Him reaching out to people with a love they don't deserve.*

    ● How is a loving God characterized by Paul in Ephesians 2:4?

    _____

    _____

    ● What has our Heavenly Father given us, according to 2 Thessalonians 2:16?

    _____

    _____

    ● Who loved whom, according to 1 John 4:10?

    _____

    _____

It's usually the first Bible verse we teach our little ones—John 3:16. "For God so loved the world that He gave His only begotten Son, that whoever believes in Him should not perish but have everlasting life" (NKJV). God loved us, even when we were sinners. God loved us so that we could love Him. God loved us so that He could give us a hope and a future.

*2. God loves each of us in a very personal way. He has known His plans for us and the path we would take for a very long time. Take a look.*

He _____ us in Him _____ the _____ of the _____, that we should be _____ and without _____ before Him in _____. —Ephesians 1:4 NKJV

[He] has _____ us and _____ us with a holy_____, not according to our _____, but according to His own _____ and _____ which was _____ to us in _____ before _____ began. —2 Timothy 1:9 NKJV

When it comes to praying for those who are without hope, we cannot help but wonder what is taking God so long to answer. If He loves them so much and has called them, why aren't they responding? But God doesn't do things according to our works or ways. He has His own plans and purposes. Only He can know why things happen the way they do. We can thank God for our own precious hope and persevere in prayer for those who still live in desperate need.

*3. Sometimes we want something to happen so badly that our prayers become incoherent. All we have is a sense of urgency and a fervent desire for God to act. At these times, how does the Holy Spirit help us to pray, according to Romans 8:26?*

_____

_____

_____

_____

_____

_____

_____

Sometimes words cannot capture the tumult we feel inside. We are left speechless when we seem to need words the most. That is when the Holy Spirit comes alongside and helps us with our prayers. His intercession on our behalf interprets our need and relays it directly to the throne of God.

*4.* **One of the most amazing prayers in our Bibles is found in John 17. In it, Jesus prays for His followers. Who does He include in this prayer, according to John 17:20?**

Imagine that! Jesus prayed for us. Many long centuries ago, Jesus had us in mind as He prayed for His followers. He knew there was a long wait ahead before His return, and He knew how far His Word would spread. Men and women the whole world over would become Christians. Perhaps His prayer will be answered in the life of your unsaved friend. Just think—you are joining Jesus in praying for their salvation.

*5.* **What does Paul tell Christians to pray for in 2 Thessalonians 3:1?**

We are accustomed to praying for many things. At a typical Wednesday night prayer meeting, we'll lift up the needs of the sick and dying. We'll pray for those who've been in accidents, for those who have travel plans, and for the financial needs of the church. But how often do we pray "that the word of the Lord may run swiftly and be glorified"? We can pray that the gospel will be spread, that ears will be opened to hear the message, and that God would be glorified by the salvation of souls.

*6. We pray for unbelievers. We pray for the spreading of the gospel. But we also pray for one another. What is Paul's prayer for us in Colossians 1:9–12?*

For this reason we also, since the day we heard it,

do not _____ to _____ for you, and to _____ that you may be _____ with the _____ of His _____ in all _____ and spiritual _____; that you may _____ _____ of the _____, fully _____ Him, being _____ in every _____ _____ and _____ in the _____ of God; _____ with all _____, according to His _____, for all _____ and _____ with _____; giving _____ to the _____.

So keep praying! Pray without ceasing! While you are waiting, turn your heart to God in prayers of intercession, and trust the Spirit to do His work.

### Praying God's Promises

We cannot make anyone else believe. That is the work of the Spirit. But we can be sure that our own lives will be found faithful by the Lord on His return. Today's prayer comes from Paul's words in 1 Corinthians 4:2–5.

*Knower of Secrets, have I been faithful? Oh, I know what other people see. I know what they think of my Sunday best behavior. But my conscience must be clear, and I'm not sure I trust my own judgment. I want to know what You think. Examine my heart, Lord. Search out the deepest places. Find out my secrets. Uncover my private motives. Have I been faithful, Lord? Amen.*

***Now it is your turn.*** We spoke of the familiarity of John 3:16 and its promise of God's great love for all people. Use it, and its surrounding context, as the basis for your Scripture prayer today.

> *And as Moses lifted up the serpent in the wilderness, even so must the Son of Man be lifted up, that whoever believes in Him should not perish but have eternal life. For God so loved the world that He gave His only begotten Son, that whoever believes in Him should not perish but have everlasting life. For God did not send His Son into the world to condemn the world, but that the world through Him might be saved. He who believes in Him is not condemned; but he who does not believe is condemned already, because he has not believed in the name of the only begotten Son of God.*
>
> John 3:14–18 NKJV

## DAY FOUR

# HOPEFUL PREPARATIONS

*"Everyone who has this hope in Him purifies himself,*
*just as He is pure."*

1 John 3:3 NKJV

Weddings—they take a lot of time and effort to pull off. There are so many decisions to make. So many details to take care of. Engagement photos, newspaper announcements, bridal showers, invitations, reserving the church, finding a reception hall, photographers, florists, caterers, rings, color schemes, bridesmaid's dresses, tuxedos, gifts, favors, menus, wedding cake, candles, special music, gift registry, programs, bridesmaids, groomsmen, best man, maid of honor, ushers, flower girls, and a ring bearer. Will you take photographs before or after the ceremony? Who will stand in the receiving line after the ceremony? When will the gift opening take place? Then we'll need a dress (ball gown, sheath, empire waist, puffed sleeve, cap sleeve, off-the-shoulder, spaghetti strap, silk, satin, organza, lace, beads, cathedral train, T-length, bustle, or bow?), shoes (glass slippers, satin finish, high heel, low heel, sling-back, pumps, or sneakers?), jewelry (diamonds, pearls, sapphires, silver, gold, or platinum?), and a veil (lace, illusion netting, organza, chin-length, shoulder-length, floor-length, hat, pill box cap, headband, wreath, or tiara?).

Getting ready for the wedding can take a whole year. Getting ready for Jesus can take a lifetime. The Bible tells us that we believers are being prepared, just like a bride, and that Jesus is our Bridegroom. When everything is ready, He'll come and take us home. Until then, we are to make ourselves ready.

*1. The church is called the bride of Christ. What is the cause for rejoicing found in Revelation 19:7?*

The Bible uses the picture of the bride and groom to describe Christ's relationship to the believers. We, the church, are the bride of Christ. We prepare ourselves for the groom's arrival, like a bride, primping and preening on her big day. Jesus is the Bridegroom. He will come to get us and take us to His home forever.

*2. The picture of a waiting bride, resplendent in pure robes and adorned with shining jewelry, is found throughout the prophetic books. Match up these examples.*

___ Isaiah 49:18     a. God will rejoice over us like a groom over his bride.

___ Isaiah 62:5     b. The Spirit and the bride say, "Come!"

___ Jeremiah 2:32     c. The New Jerusalem is being prepared like a bride.

___ Revelation 21:2     d. A bride dresses with care and binds on ornaments.

___ Revelation 21:9     e. "Come, I will show you the bride, the Lamb's wife."

___ Revelation 22:17     f. A bride could never forget all her fripperies.

When it comes to her wedding day, a bride is all about details. That one day is the culmination of months of planning. She wants to make sure everything is just right, from the flower arrangements to the shade of nail polish on her toes.

*3. Isaiah compares the preparations God makes in our hearts with the preparations that a bride and her groom make on their wedding day. With what does God clothe us, according to Isaiah 61:10?*

_____

_____

_____

_____

_____

Our hopeful preparations don't have much to do with manicures and mud baths. We aren't making external preparations for Christ's coming.

All our efforts are focused on internal things. After all, "The LORD does not see as man sees; for man looks at the outward appearance, but the LORD looks at the heart" (1 Sam. 16:7 NKJV). We are clothed with salvation, and robed with righteousness. That is the loveliness that most pleases the Lord.

*4. Before you can put on the pretty clothes of a bride, you want to be all clean underneath. What purifies our hearts, according to 1 Peter 1:22?*

_____

_____

_____

_____

_____

_____

God showed His people that they could exude His holy characteristic in their everyday lives. That's why God gave Moses specific laws for His people so they would be set apart from the nations living around them. Leviticus is full of them—it's a list of commonplace details to govern their lives in holiness. We too can show that we've been "set apart" in holiness, by doing what is just, loving our spouses, showing mercy to all, walking humbly before God, honoring our parents, not stealing, and so on. Nothing mystical, but it sets us apart from the world and shows them that we are different. A righteous woman has her heart made holy by Jesus and lives out her days in a way that sets her apart from the crowd.

*5. Once the dress is in place, all the other adornments are added. Scripture talks about the things that should adorn the lives of God's people.*

• What does Psalm 93:5 say adorns the house of the Lord?

_____

_____

● What kinds of finery are described in Ezekiel 16:11–13?

_____

_____

● How did women in ancient times adorn themselves, according to 1 Peter 3:5?

_____

_____

Our time of waiting for the hope of our hearts to be fulfilled is time we can use to prepare for that day. You wouldn't want to be caught on your wedding day with dirt under your nails, unwashed hair, or wearing your rattiest underwear, would you? Well, neither would you want to be caught unprepared when Jesus comes for you. We would want to make ourselves lovely in His sight. "You should be known for the beauty that comes from within, the unfading beauty of a gentle and quiet spirit, which is so precious to God" (1 Pet. 3:4 NLT).

*6. While we are making preparations in our hearts for Jesus' coming, what preparation is our Bridegroom making for us? Paul gives us a hint in 1 Corinthians 2:9.*

_____

_____

_____

_____

_____

_____

You trust Jesus, "because of the hope which is laid up for you in heaven" (Col. 1:5 NKJV). It is a living hope. It is an eternal hope. And it will be more wonderful than anything we could ever imagine—and some of us have pretty good imaginations! So in our eagerness to see that hope revealed, we prepare ourselves to receive it. Our hope-filled preparations adorn our hearts with righteousness and gentleness. And these make it possible for us to hope and wait quietly for the Lord.

### PRAYING GOD'S PROMISES

We must be prepared for the Coming of Jesus. In Revelations, the Lord sent letters to the churches, telling them their areas of weakness and urging them to shore them up before it was too late. One of these letters is the basis for today's Scripture prayer—Revelation 3:1–5.

*Eagerly Expected One, You know me better than anyone ever will. You know when my heart is receptive to Your Word and Your will. And You know when it is hard as stone. I am so weak in some areas of my life, help me to strengthen them before they lead me astray again. Remind me of what I already know. Teach me to call sin a sin and to repent quickly. I will hold fast to hope. I will watch for Your coming. I know the signs, and I will not be caught off guard. Though I don't know when the time will be, I will live in a state of constant preparedness. I'll be ready for You! Then You will clothe me in white garments, and introduce me to Your Father before all the angels of heaven. Oh, I'll be ready! Amen.*

Jesus is indeed the perfect Man. He cares about what you think. He loves you for your mind! He loves you for the hidden person of your heart! Take the two verses in the margin as your inspiration, and journal a prayer of preparation here.

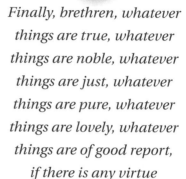

*Finally, brethren, whatever things are true, whatever things are noble, whatever things are just, whatever things are pure, whatever things are lovely, whatever things are of good report, if there is any virtue and if there is anything praiseworthy—meditate on these things.*

Philippians 4:8 NKJV

*Do not let your adornment be merely outward— arranging the hair, wearing gold, or putting on fine apparel—rather let it be the hidden person of the heart, with the incorruptible beauty of a gentle and quiet spirit, which is very precious in the sight of God.*

1 Peter 3:3, 4 NKJV

## DAY FIVE

# HOPE AND WAIT QUIETLY

*"It is good that one should hope and wait quietly*
*for the salvation of the LORD."*
Lamentations 3:26 NKJV

Dogs are a perfect example of watchfulness. We have two—a pair of Chihuahua puppies named Timothy and Titus. They go about their business, sniffing and scratching and sleeping, until something alerts them. A scent or a sound out of the ordinary. Then, they sit straight, prick up their ears, and sniff the air. Should any stranger dare knock on our front door, speak within hearing range, or cut across our backyard, they are assaulted by the fierce yaps of our little watchdogs. Who knew such small dogs could make so much noise? Another excellent example of watchfulness would be little children waiting for their daddy to get home from work. In fine weather, they're lined up on the front step. In foul weather, their noses are pressed against the window glass. They strain their ears for the sound of oncoming vehicles, or they send up a shout every time headlights come into view. "Is it him? Is it him?" I also know the eagerness that the end of a workday brings. My ears are tuned to the sound of our car's engine, which I can easily pick out from among those of our neighbors'. I know the sound of footsteps on the walk. I recognize the jingle of keys and the turning of the lock on the front door. I know the creak of the floorboard in the foyer and the sound of feet on the steps. Our ears are tuned to the sounds we've come to recognize apart from all others. We listen for those that are most familiar and dear to us.

In this same way, we watch and wait for Jesus to return. When He comes to fulfill every hope, will you be caught listening for the sound of His call?

*1.* **Consider this fact—God's plans will succeed. The ending to our story has already been written. He's thought of every detail, and when everything has played itself out, all of us will stand in awe at His wisdom and sovereignty. How does Paul put it in Ephesians 3:14?**

When I think of the _____ and _____
of God's _____, I _____ to my
_____ and _____ to the _____.
—Ephesians 3:14 NLT

God is sovereign. We can trust Him to handle things. But He has entrusted us with certain responsibilities in the meantime. We have important roles to play in His plans. We have work to do, "as unto the Lord." We have husbands to help and children to raise up "in the nurture and admonition of the Lord." We have bosses to respect. We have promises to keep. We have laws to obey. We have brothers and sisters in the faith to love and encourage. We have acquaintances who have never heard the Good News. We have loved ones, wandering far from the Lord, to pray for. Our waiting is not wasted time.

*2.* **Until our hope comes, we have things to do. As Jesus put it in one of His parables, "Do business till I come" (Luke 19:13 NKJV). What kind of business would that be, according to Paul in 1 Thessalonians 4:11?**

When the Bible says to "do business" until Jesus' return, the Greek word is pragma, from which we get our English word pragmatic. It literally means to "keep busy," or "to work." Jesus says to keep busy doing His work until He comes back. It's not busy work, though. The work of the Lord is meaningful, practical, and sensible. We aren't to be busybodies, doing senseless stuff to fill our time. As believers, we'll be busy doing things that are meaningful to God and practical for the advancement of His kingdom.

*3. What is Paul's confident statement concerning the return of his Savior in 2 Timothy 1:12?*

We have stored up our treasures in heaven. The people who have been led to salvation because of our words and our efforts. The monies we have given in faithful stewardship. The time we sacrifice for the kingdom. Worship from a thankful heart. The use of our gifts. Our attitude of joyful perseverance. The fruit of the Spirit displayed in our daily lives. The hours we have spent in intercessory prayer. Anything that we have done for the Lord has been stored up in heaven. Those small sacrifices that no one else ever saw—they are remembered. When we give God our best, He rewards us in eternal ways.

*4. Some things are left in God's hands, and some things are left into our own keeping. What kinds of things are we urged to keep while we wait? Match them up.*

___ Ephesians 4:3    a. Keep God's commandments because you love Him.

___ 1 Timothy 5:22    b. Keep yourself pure.

___ 1 Timothy 6:14    c. Keep the words of this book and worship God.

___ James 1:27    d. Keep yourself blameless by obeying God's commands.

___ 1 John 5:3    e. Keep yourself from idols.

___ 1 John 5:21    f. Keep the unity of the Spirit in the bond of peace.

___ Revelation 1:3    g. Keep yourself unspotted by the world.

___ Revelation 22:9    h. Keep the Word of God, which you have read and heard.

Almost every one of those verses carries the same basic message. Keep yourself pure by keeping God's commandments. Keep yourself blameless. Do it because you love God. Do it because God said so. Those who are waiting with expectation and eagerness are the same people who take God seriously. They hear His words and act upon them. They are preparing for the hope that is to come.

*5. Jesus' urgent exhortation comes in Mark 13:37: "And what I say to you, I say to all: Watch!" We are to be watchful people, anticipating our Lord's return with eagerness and diligence.*

● Matthew 25:13—Watch because

_____

_____

- Mark 13:33—Watch and pray because

_____

_____

- Mark 13:35—Watch because it could be

_____

_____

- 1 Thessalonians 5:6—Watch and be

_____

_____

Get the message? Watch! Don't be caught napping! Don't get so comfortable that you become careless. It's far too easy to let down our guard where sin and temptation are concerned. So watch, acting as if you're fully awake and alert to what is going on in our hearts and around us. Also, be sober! Sober? Sober-minded people are temperate and moderate. They are in control of themselves and are able to keep their natural lusts and cravings in check. So watch and be sober until the Lord comes.

_6._ **Our hope is nearer than we might think, and the reward it brings with it will be greater than anything this world could offer.**

- How long shall we hope in the Lord, according to Psalm 131:3?

_____

_____

- What does the brother of Jesus urge us to do in Jude 21?

_____

_____

• Whom does Jesus call blessed in Luke 12:37?

_____

_____

Blessed is the woman who, when her Master comes for her, is found watching for His approach. Her ears are tuned for the sound of His voice, of His step, of His hand on the doorknob. He might come at any moment. In hopes of His imminent arrival, she'd set the table and put a light in the window. The supper is simmering in the crockpot, ready at a moment's notice. There's a loaf on the breadboard and a pie in the pantry. A jelly jar filled with flowers graces the center of the table. It's simple, but everything is neat, clean, and thoughtfully prepared. She's just finished folding a load of dishtowels, warm from the dryer when a distant, but familiar, sound reaches her ears. Her Lord has returned! Finding the lady faithfully watching for Him, He invites her to join Him. He dishes up dinner for two, and they spend the rest of the evening catching up on all their news, face-to-face.

## PRAYING GOD'S PROMISES

All of God's Word will come to pass, just as He said it would. Today's Scripture prayer comes from 2 Peter 1:19, where the enthusiastic apostle reminds us that he saw messianic prophecies coming true right before his very eyes.

_Living Word, You are eternal and true. Your Word has been faithfully passed down to us. The writers of Scripture were moved by the Spirit. They were Your men, set apart for the task of recording Your words. What a miracle! Not one word—one jot or tittle—of Your prophecies will be missed in the end. Everything will come to pass, just as You said it would. Your prophecies will all be confirmed. They have shown a light into dark places. They have given us a hope beyond anything we could imagine. And one day soon, the day will dawn as Your morning star rises in our hearts. Come quickly, Lord! Amen._

God will give us the strength to do what we know is good and right. It is He who will enable us to watch and wait quietly for the wonderful hope that lies just ahead. For your Scripture prayer today, use 2 Timothy 3:14–17 as you journal.

*But you must continue in the things which you have learned and been assured of, knowing from whom you have learned them, and that from childhood you have known the Holy Scriptures, which are able to make you wise for salvation through faith which is in Christ Jesus. All Scripture is given by inspiration of God, and is profitable for doctrine, for reproof, for correction, for instruction in righteousness, that the man of God may be complete, thoroughly equipped for every good work.*

2 Timothy 3:14–17 NKJV

## CONCLUSION

Consider Job's words for a moment in Job 8:13–14 (NKJV):

*So are the paths of all who forget God;*
*And the hope of the hypocrite shall perish,*
*Whose confidence shall be cut off,*
*And whose trust is a spider's web.*

When people try to live apart from God, they have no life at all. If they make a good show of faith to hide their hypocritical heart, they are doomed. What is their hope compared to? A spider's web—delicate, fragile, and tenuous. Now consider again the words found in Hebrews 6:19 (NKJV):

*This hope we have as an anchor of the soul,*
*both sure and steadfast,*
*and which enters the Presence behind the veil.*

When people have placed their trust in God, their life is forever secure. What is our hope compared to? An anchor—trustworthy, solid, and sure. Our steadfast hope anchors our hearts to heaven.

We have faith, love, joy, and peace. We shall persevere and hope until the end. We are being prepared for Christ's coming. And we remain busy about the Lord's work in the meantime. Be Ready! Watch! Hope!

## JOURNALING SUGGESTIONS

What kinds of days are the hardest in which to remain steady and consistent? What are the little things that seem to trip you up and set you off most often? Are they things that hope can strengthen you to face?

Do you avoid telling people about Jesus because you just don't know what to say? Set a timer for three minutes, and write down as many things that you can think of about God and Jesus. Look at that! Are these things you could tell a searching friend?

Who are you praying for right now—someone who needs salvation? Why not write to the Lord about them in your journal. Spill out your prayers for them there.

Whole books have been written to help a bride-to-be prepare for her big day. What kinds of items do you think would show up in the checklists of the bride of the Lamb?

We are urged to watch for the Lord's coming. What kinds of things epitomize watchfulness to you? Make a list. Then, choose something on the list to serve as a reminder of the Hope for which you are waiting and watching. Put it in a prominent place in your home to help you keep your thoughts fixed on God. It will be just a trinket to remind you of the great treasure that lies in store.

## JOURNALING QUOTE

*My journal is my constant companion.*
*It is never far from my reach. It goes to church*
*with me; accompanies me on any excursion,*
*fun, or work; it waits for me in the mornings*
*beside my bed or on my desk; and it calls to me*
*in the middle of a hectic day.*

Nicole Johnson

# LEADER'S GUIDE ANSWERS

## LESSON 1

### DAY ONE

*1.* All of us would like to have a life that is characterized by most, if not all, of the qualities in this list. What's more, most of us would have to admit that we respect and admire people who are characterized by these qualities. But all of our efforts to be "good" will not sway the God who sees the heart. He has a different criterion in mind, and without it, even the most likeable person is hopeless.

*2.* "Speak to all the congregation of the children of Israel, and say to them: 'You shall be holy, for I the LORD your God am holy' " (Lev. 19:2 NKJV). God expects nothing less than holiness. Such sinless perfection is beyond the scope of our human abilities.

*3.* "As it is written: 'There is none righteous, no, not one; There is none who understands; There is none who seeks after God. They have all turned aside; They have together become unprofitable; There is none who does good, no, not one' " (Rom. 3:10–12 NKJV). None of us can ever achieve righteousness on our own. None of us can achieve perfection. Without Jesus, we can never be holy.

*4.* "We know that the law's commands are for those who have the law. This stops all excuses and brings the whole world under God's judgment, because no one can be made right with God by following the law. The law only shows us our sin" (Rom. 3:19, 20 NCV). Thanks to God's laws, none of us has any excuses. We all understand how we have sinned and what the consequences should be.

*5.* "For whoever shall keep the whole law, and yet stumble in one point, he is guilty of all" (James 2:10 NKJV). With God, it's all or nothing. He doesn't make exceptions or accept a majority report. You are either a sinner or you're not.

*6.* "The law made nothing perfect; on the other hand, there is the bringing in of a better hope, through which we draw near to God" (Heb. 7:19 NKJV). Nothing could be redeemed by the law itself. That only pointed out how far we had fallen. But God brought us something we were desperately lacking—hope. The hope that we could draw near to God.

### DAY TWO

*1.* "A man is justified by faith apart from the deeds of the law" (Rom. 3:28 NKJV)—contrasts faith and works. "For what the law could not do. . .God did by sending His own Son" (Rom. 8:3 NKJV)—contrasts the Law and Jesus. "Us who do not walk according to the flesh but according to the Spirit" (Rom. 8:4 NKJV)—contrasts the Spirit and the flesh. "In Christ Jesus you who once were far off have been brought near" (Eph. 2:13 NKJV)—contrasts near and far. "For you were once darkness, but now you are light in the Lord" (Eph. 5:8 NKJV)—contrasts light and dark. "Who once were not a people but are now the people of God, who had not obtained mercy but now have obtained mercy" (1 Pet. 2:10 NKJV)—contrasts those who belong to God and have been given mercy with those who have not.

*2.* "Before I was born, the LORD called me to serve him. The LORD named me while I was still in my mother's body" (Is. 49:1 NCV). God called Isaiah even before he was born. "God had special plans for me and set me apart for his work even before I was born. He called me through his grace" (Gal. 1:15 NCV). God had special plans for Paul's life. "God called me to be an apostle and chose me to tell the Good News" (Rom. 1:1 NCV). God's plans for Paul were for the spreading of the gospel. "I, therefore, the prisoner of the Lord, beseech you to walk worthy of the calling with which you were called" (Eph. 4:1 NKJV). Paul's plea is for believers to be worthy of the calling that they have received.

*3.* "When we were utterly helpless, Christ came at just the right time and died for us sinners. Now, no one is likely to die for a good person, though someone might be willing to die for a person who is especially good. But God showed his great love for us by sending Christ to die for us while we were still sinners" (Rom. 5:6–8 NLT). Jesus came on our behalf, not because we were good, but to make us good. Before we could even call ourselves His friends, He was willing to lay down His life for us. What amazing love!

*4.* a, c, d, b

*5.* "You will seek the Lord your God, and you will find Him" (Deut. 4:29 NKJV). If we seek God, we will find Him. "You will seek Me and find Me, when you search for Me with all your heart" (Jer. 29:13 NKJV). When we search for God, it must be wholehearted pursuit. Only then will we find the Lord. "They should seek the Lord, in the hope that they might grope for Him and find Him, though He is not far from each one of us" (Acts 17:27 NKJV). God is never far from us. He shows Himself to those who earnestly seek Him.

## DAY THREE

*1.* David says, "The LORD is all I need. He takes care of me" (Ps. 16:5 NCV). It's not as if choosing God means that everything else will be taken away from us. God is the provider of everything we really need. David knew that the Lord would be enough, because God had promised to take care of him. Paul writes, "And He said to me, 'My grace is sufficient for you, for My strength is made perfect in weakness' " (2 Cor. 12:9 NKJV). Of course we feel insufficient for the task set before us—we are! But God helps us along our way, and we can give Him the glory for it. Paul's message assures us that the Lord will be enough. Grace is enough. God's strength is enough. Philippians 4:19 assures us that "God shall supply all your need according to His riches in glory by Christ Jesus" (NKJV). In Colossians 2:10, Paul tells us, "you are complete in Him" (NKJV). Other translations say that we will have "a full and true life" (NCV) and that "fullness comes together for you" (MSG).

*2.* "The LORD will give grace and glory; No good thing will He withhold from those who walk uprightly" (Ps. 84:11 NKJV). God gives grace, glory, and good things. "If you then, being evil, know how to give good gifts to your children, how much more will your Father who is in heaven give what is good to those who ask Him!" (Matt. 7:11 NASB). Good things are ours if we ask for them. God knows what is good, and gives those things as gifts to His children. Jesus says that "it is your Father's good pleasure to give you the kingdom" (Luke 12:32 NKJV). It pleases Him to give. And James reminds us that "every good gift and every perfect gift is from above" (James 1:17 NKJV).

*3.* The psalm says, "The LORD takes pleasure in those who fear Him, in those who hope in His mercy" (Ps. 147:11 NLT). We hope for mercy. Solomon says, "The hope of the righteous will be gladness" (Prov. 10:28 NLT). We will rejoice when our hope is realized. And Jeremiah tells the Lord, "You are my hope in the day of doom" (Jer. 17:17 NLT). Only God can save us. He is our only hope.

*4.* "The eyes of your understanding being enlightened; that you may know what is the hope of His calling, what are the riches of the glory of His inheritance in the saints, and what is the exceeding greatness of His power toward us who believe" (Eph. 1:18, 19 NKJV). Paul says that

our hope comes with great riches—an inheritance—and with great power.

*5.* "In hope of eternal life which God, who cannot lie, promised before time began" (Titus 1:2 NKJV). Eternal life. None of us wants to die in sin and be separated from God forever. We want to live. We want to live forever. We long for eternal life in the presence of God.

*6.* "Christ in you, the hope of glory" (Col. 1:27 NKJV). What are we hoping for? The hope of glory! We want to live forever. We want to go to heaven. We want to be with God.

*7.* "Because I have done what is right, I will see you. When I awake, I will be fully satisfied, for I will see you face to face" (Ps. 17:15 NLT). David's dearest desire was to see his Lord face to face. Just like us, David was looking forward to an eternity in heaven with God.

## DAY FOUR

*1.* "Through Christ you have come to trust in God. And because God raised Christ from the dead and gave him great glory, your faith and hope can be placed confidently in God" (1 Pet. 1:20, 21 NLT). Our hope can be placed in God with confidence because of what He did. He raised Jesus from the dead.

*2.* IF there is no resurrection of the dead, THEN Christ is not risen. IF Jesus is not risen, THEN our preaching has been empty. IF our preaching is empty, THEN our faith is empty. IF Christ is not risen, THEN our faith is futile. IF believers are still in their sins, THEN when they die, they will perish. IF hope in Christ is not for eternal life, THEN we are of all men, most pitiable.

*3.* f, d, h, g, a, c, b, e

*4.* "For you were bought at a price; therefore glorify God in your body and in your spirit, which are God's" (1 Cor. 6:20 NKJV).

*5.* According to verse 13, on what does our hope rest? On Jesus and the grace He brought. How are we to behave ourselves, according to verse 14? Obediently, rather than following our own selfish desires. Why, according to verses 15 and 16? Because we have been called by a holy God, and He desires us to be holy as well. Who is Peter talking to in verse 17? "Those who call on the Father"—in other words, believers. How should we conduct ourselves, according to verse 17? With fear. What was the cost of our redemption, according to verse 19? The precious blood of Christ. Who did Jesus come for, according to verse 20? For "you who believe"—that's us! What did God do for Jesus in verse 21? God raised Jesus from the dead. Why (or "so that"), according to verse 21? So that we would have faith in God and hope for eternal life. Because of all this ("since"), we should do what, according to verse 22? We should love one another. And how was the incorruptible seed planted, according to verse 23? Through the Word of God.

*6.* "Christ died for all so that those who live would not continue to live for themselves. He died for them and was raised from the dead so that they would live for him (2 Cor. 5:15 NCV). Paul says, "I died to the law so that I can now live for God" (Gal. 2:19 NCV). Jesus "bore our sins in His own body on the tree, that we, having died to sins, might live for righteousness" (1 Pet. 2:24 NKJV).

## DAY FIVE

*1.* "These are written that you may believe that Jesus is the Christ, the Son of God, and that believing you may have life in His name" (John 20:31 NKJV). Did you see that? John wrote those things down so that we could have life, and eternal life is the hope we hold on to!

*2.* "Prophecy never came by the will of man, but holy men of God spoke as they were moved by the Holy Spirit" (2 Pet. 1:21 NKJV).

*3.* "All Scripture is given by inspiration of God, and is profitable for doctrine, for reproof, for correction, for instruction in righteousness, that the man of God may be complete, thoroughly equipped for every good work" (2 Tim. 3:16, 17 NKJV). The literal translation of that first phrase would be, "All Scripture is God-breathed."

*4.* Psalm 31:3—You are my rock and my fortress. Psalm 31:4—You are my strength. Psalm 32:7—You are my hiding place. Psalm 40:17—You are my help and my deliverer. Psalm 71:5—You are my hope. You are my trust. Psalm 71:7—You are my strong refuge. Psalm 119:57—You are my portion.

*5.* "For this reason I will not be negligent to remind you always of these things, though you know and are established in the present truth. Yes, I think it is right, as long as I am in this tent, to stir you up by reminding you, knowing that shortly I must put off my tent, just as our Lord Jesus Christ showed me. Moreover I will be careful to ensure that you always have a reminder of these things after my decease" (2 Pet. 1:12–15 NKJV). Did you see that? He said "reminder" three times! Even if you're "established in the . . . truth," keep the Word in front of your eyes. To do otherwise would be negligent!

*6.* "For me to write the same things to you is not tedious, but for you it is safe" (Phil. 3:1 NKJV). We need to hear the truth again and again. We need to be reminded, encouraged, and urged on in our faith. The Bible is where we can turn for God's wisdom and truth. For us, it is safe—not tedious—to return to the Word again and again.

# LESSON 2

## DAY ONE

*1.* "When I tried to keep the law, I realized I could never earn God's approval. So I died to the law so that I might live for God. I have been crucified with Christ" (Gal. 2:19 NLT). Paul had tried very hard to earn God's approval, but when faced with Jesus' sacrifice and God's gift of grace, Paul "died to the law."

*2.* "Seek the LORD, all you meek of the earth, who have upheld His justice. Seek righteousness, seek humility" (Zeph. 2:3 NKJV). The prophet urges God's people to seek three things: the Lord, righteousness, and humility. "He has shown you, O man, what is good; and what does the LORD require of you but to do justly, to love mercy, and to walk humbly with your God?" (Mic. 6:8 NKJV). According to this passage, God requires us to do what is right, love mercy, and walk humbly with Him. "Therefore humble yourselves under the mighty hand of God, that He may exalt you in due time" (1 Pet. 5:6 NKJV). And lastly, the psalmist says, "The LORD takes pleasure in His people; He will beautify the humble with salvation" (Ps. 149:4 NKJV).

*3.* The fill-in-the-blank answers are as follows. Salvation comes by grace. We are saved through faith. Not of yourselves. It is the gift of God. Not of works. Lest anyone should boast.

*4.* e, g, b, d, a, h, f, c. Just as Paul says, "He died for our sins, just as God our Father planned, in order to rescue us from this evil world in which we live" (Gal. 1:4 NLT).

*5.* Paul says, "God is faithful" (1 Cor. 1:9 NKJV). When the Lord says that we have hope through Him, we can be confident that we shall see that hope fulfilled. David says, "The testimony of the LORD is sure" (Ps. 19:7 NKJV). God's Word is sure—true, dependable, trustworthy. These are the basis for our confidence and our hope. God is faithful, and His promises are sure.

*6.* Deuteronomy 31:6—He is the One who goes with you. Deuteronomy 32:4—He is the Rock. Psalm 24:10—He is the King of glory. Psalm 28:8—He is the saving refuge.

Ephesians 5:23—He is the Savior of the body. Colossians 1:15—He is the image of the invisible God, the first-born over all creation. Colossians 1:18—He is the head of the body, the beginning, the firstborn from the dead. Hebrews 9:15—He is the Mediator.

## DAY TWO

*1.* "They do not know, nor do they understand; they walk about in darkness" (Ps. 82:5 NKJV). People who do not know God are stumbling around in the darkness. "My people have been lost sheep. Their shepherds have led them astray; they have turned them away" (Jer. 50:6 NKJV). People who have no hope will follow just about anyone in their desperation to find purpose for their existence. Sadly, they put their hopes into the hands of those who will only lead them falsely. "What profit is it to a man if he gains the whole world, and is himself destroyed or lost?" (Luke 9:25 NKJV). Even people who seem to have their life pulled together—nice families, good friends, thriving businesses, beautiful homes, admirable goals—have nothing in the end if they don't know Jesus. They will lose everything that is passing anyhow, but they will lose an eternity with God as well.

*2.* "The Son of Man has come to save that which was lost" (Matt. 18:11 NKJV). He came for the lost. "I am the light of the world. He who follows Me shall not walk in darkness, but have the light of life" (John 8:12 NKJV). He brings light to those who wander in the dark.

*3.* In the "before" column, we find such phrases as "shuffling along," "eyes on the ground," and "absorbed." It's very easy to become so distracted by our own life that we let it hold all our attention. We live as if we have blinders on, unaware of God or others. Such a life is very self-centered. However, in the "after" column, we should have written such phrases as "looking up," "alert," "eyes on Christ," and "seeing things from His perspective." Jesus gives us hope, and along with that He gives us a new perspective—a new way of seeing things.

*4.* "Your attitude should be the same that Christ Jesus had" (Phil. 2:5 NLT). All we need to do is look at the life of Jesus to find out what our lives should look like! "Your task is to single-mindedly serve Christ. Do that and you'll kill two birds with one stone: pleasing the God above you and proving your worth" (Rom. 14:18 MSG). Our lives should be spent in aiming to please God. "May God, who gives this patience and encouragement, help you live in complete harmony with each other—each with the atti-tude of Christ Jesus toward the other" (Rom. 15:5 NLT). In order to display a Christlike attitude toward one another, we need God's patience and encouragement!

*5.* Paul says, "I press toward the goal for the prize of the upward call of God in Christ Jesus" (Phil. 3:14 NKJV). Paul presses on because he wants to gain eternal life with Jesus. That one goal is always before his eyes. It is his greatest hope. In 1 Corinthians, Paul compares life to a race, and urges all of us to "run in such a way that you may obtain" the prize. Take it seriously. Apply yourself. The hope is worth the effort to reach it. "They do it to obtain a perishable crown, but we for an imperishable crown" (1 Cor. 9:25 NKJV). So many people waste their efforts chasing after passing glories. Paul urges us on, because our goal in Christ is an imperishable one.

*6.* "I would have lost heart, unless I had believed that I would see the goodness of the Lord in the land of the living" (Ps. 27:13 NKJV). Our hopes are not limited to our perspectives, our attitudes, and our goals. We don't have to wait for glory in order to see hope realized in our lives. David understood this and thanked God for the bless-ings that he enjoyed from the Lord's hand in his every-day life. Without them, David admits that he might have lost heart—given up hope.

## DAY THREE

*1.* "Wash me thoroughly from my iniquity, and cleanse me from my sin" (Ps. 51:2 NKJV). David knows enough to turn to God for forgiveness and cleansing. "You, being dead in your trespasses and the uncircumcision of your flesh, He has made alive together with Him, having for-given you all trespasses" (Col. 2:13 NKJV). "If we confess our sins, He is faithful and just to forgive us our sins and to cleanse us from all unrighteousness" (1 John 1:9 NKJV).

*2.* "Your ears shall hear a word behind you, saying, 'This is the way, walk in it,' whenever you turn to the right hand or whenever you turn to the left" (Is. 30:21 NKJV). Who wouldn't love to know exactly what to choose, where to turn, what direction to take? A heart tuned to God, who knows what His Word says and trusts His instructions, will be shown what to do.

*3.* c, a, e, f, b, d

*4.* "Bend down, O Lord, and hear my prayer; answer me, for I need your help" (Ps. 86:1 NLT). "I took my troubles to the Lord; I cried out to him, and he answered my prayer" (Ps. 120:1 NLT). "Call to Me, and I will answer you, and show you great and mighty things, which you do not know" (Jer. 33:3 NKJV). "He shall call upon Me, and I will answer him; I will be with him in trouble; I will deliver him and honor him" (Ps. 91:15 NKJV). "I, the Lord, am the one who answers your prayers and watches over you" (Hos. 14:8 NCV).

*5.* Jeremiah 31:3—We are loved with an everlasting love. Matthew 28:20—We are never alone. Luke 12:22—We don't have to worry about life; God provides for our needs. John 14:26—We have been given the Holy Spirit as a Helper. John 14:27—We have peace. We don't need to be afraid. John 15:15—We are counted as friends of Jesus. 1 Thessalonians 4:13, 14—We do not face death with sadness, because Jesus will raise all believers again. 2 Peter 1:4—God has made us great and precious promises, which He will always keep.

# DAY FOUR

*1.* "David spoke to the leaders of the Levites to appoint their brethren to be the singers accompanied by instruments of music, stringed instruments, harps, and cymbals, by raising the voice with resounding joy" (1 Chr. 15:16 NKJV). David planned for the rejoicing of God's people. He wrote music, he hired a band, and he coached the singers. "The people played the flutes and rejoiced with great joy, so that the earth seemed to split with their sound" (1 Kin. 1:40 NKJV). Deafening! "That day they offered great sacrifices, and rejoiced, for God had made them rejoice with great joy; the women and the children also rejoiced, so that the joy of Jerusalem was heard afar off" (Neh. 12:43 NKJV). Even from a long way off, the joy of God's people could be heard.

*2.* c, f, h, a, j, d, g, k, e, i, b

*3.* "Be glad in the LORD and rejoice, you righteous; and shout for joy, all you upright in heart!" (Ps. 32:11 NKJV). Joyful people are characterized as those who are righteous and upright in heart. "God gives wisdom and knowledge and joy to a man who is good in His sight" (Eccl. 2:26 NKJV). God grants blessings to those who are good in His sight. And not only joy, but wisdom and knowledge as well. "The humble also shall increase their joy in the LORD" (Is. 29:19 NKJV). God lifts up the poor and gives joy to the humble.

*4.* "Do not sorrow, for the joy of the LORD is your strength" (Neh. 8:10 NKJV). Joy is our strength. What does that mean?

*5.* Psalm 43:4—David refers to God as his "exceeding joy" (NKJV). Jeremiah 15:16—God's Word is a source of joy. John 17:13—Jesus' words and presence in this world are a source of joy. Acts 13:52—The Holy Spirit brings joy. 1 John 1:4—Again, Scripture brings joy. 3 John 1:4—Joy

comes in knowing that our children (biological or spiritual) are also walking with the Lord.

*6.* "In Your presence is fullness of joy; at Your right hand are pleasures forevermore" (Ps. 16:11 NKJV). Fullness of joy is in God's presence. "His lord said to him, 'Well done, good and faithful servant. . .Enter into the joy of your lord" (Matt. 25:21 NKJV). Those are the words we are all waiting to hear. Someday, we will enter into joy.

# DAY FIVE

*1.* d, g, e, b, i, a, c, h, j, f

*2.* "Those who know Your name will put their trust in You; for You, LORD, have not forsaken those who seek You" (Ps. 9:10 NKJV). The New Century Version puts it this way: "Those who know the LORD trust him, because he will not leave those who come to him." If you know God, you'll trust Him. When you trust Him, He'll never forsake you—He'll never let you down.

*3.* "You are my hope, O Lord GOD; You are my trust from my youth" (Ps. 71:5 NKJV). David had always trusted the Lord, and had placed his life in God's hands from the time he was a boy. "As for God, His way is perfect; The word of the LORD is proven; He is a shield to all who trust in Him" (2 Sam. 22:31 NKJV). God's way is a perfect way. God's Word is a proven word. Those who trust in Him will not be disappointed. "For to this end we both labor and suffer reproach, because we trust in the living God" (1 Tim. 4:10 NKJV). Even though it wasn't an easy path, Paul trusted that God had set him on the right path. "Keep my soul, and deliver me; let me not be ashamed, for I put my trust in You" (Ps. 25:20 NKJV). David trusted the Lord with all he had and all he was—right down to his own soul.

*4.* "The LORD is good, a stronghold in the day of trouble; and He knows those who trust in Him" (Nah. 1:7 NKJV). It hardly matters what you can convince others to think about you. Your spiritual condition is known by your Heavenly Father, and you are answerable to Him for it. He knows when we're leaning on something other than Him. And sometimes, He'll let us learn how futile that is the hard way.

*5.* In Psalm 36:7, the people trust in the Lord because they have known His lovingkindness. In Psalm 37:5, those who trust themselves into the Lord's hands will see Him bring everything to pass. According to The Message, "He'll do whatever needs to be done." In Psalm 52:8, David says that he trusts in God's mercy. And in

Psalm 56:3, we discover that trust is able to dispel our fears.

*6.* The psalmist is drawn to God's quality of lovingkindness. It is this that strengthens his trust in the Lord. Next, the psalmist clearly states that he trusts in God. Because of this trust, he is willing to do as God asks, walking along the path that God chooses. And lastly, the writer trusts God with his soul. In this case, he's probably talking more about baring his soul to God, being vulnerable through prayer. Though one could infer that the psalmist would also be placing his life into God's hands.

# LESSON 3
## DAY ONE

*1.* "We were saved, and we have this hope. If we see what we are waiting for, that is not really hope. People do not hope for something they already have. But we are hoping for something we do not have yet, and we are waiting for it patiently" (Rom. 8:24, 25 NCV). Now that makes good sense. Of course we can't see our hope—if we could, we wouldn't be waiting for it anymore. It wouldn't be hope. It would be here.

*2.* "We walk by faith, not by sight" (2 Cor. 5:7 NKJV). Just as hope could not be hope if we could see it now, faith would not be faith if it didn't depend on the invisible. We walk by faith. That is our calling.

*3.* "Now to the King eternal, immortal, invisible" (1 Tim. 1:17 NKJV). This verse brings to mind the familiar hymn: "Immortal, invisible, God only wise. In light, inaccessible, hid from our eyes." In the familiar hope chapter, we read about Moses' faith: "He endured as seeing Him who is invisible" (Heb. 11:27 NKJV). Moses' faith in God was so great, he lived as if he could see God. "Since the creation of the world His invisible attributes are clearly seen" (Rom. 1:20 NKJV). Although God is invisible, He reveals things about Himself to us in creation.

*4.* "I've built this splendid temple, O God, to mark your invisible presence forever" (1 Kin. 8:13 MSG). The temple was a place for God to dwell on this earth. It was a place for God's people to meet with Him for worship.

*5.* f, c, e, a, d, g, b

*6.* "He is the image of the invisible God, the firstborn over all creation" (Col. 1:15 NKJV). We cannot see God, but Jesus came as Emmanuel, "God with us." Suddenly, the divine was someone who could be seen, touched, heard.

## DAY TWO

*1.* "Behold, how good and how pleasant it is for brethren to dwell together in unity" (Ps. 133:1 NKJV). Peaceful cohabitation. Cooperation. Unity of mind and purpose. Teamwork.

*2.* "Holy Father, keep through Your name those whom You have given Me, that they may be one as We are" (John 17:11 NKJV). Jesus prayed that we would be one—united. "That they may be one just as We are one" (John 17:22 NKJV). Our relationship mirrors that of Jesus and His Heavenly Father. "That the world may believe that You sent Me" (John 17:21 NKJV). Our unity serves to show the world that we belong to Christ and have been changed by Him.

*3.* "Do all these things; but most important, love each other. Love is what holds you all together in perfect unity" (Col. 3:14 NCV). According to Paul, love was the most important thing. Why? Because love is what holds us together and engenders unity.

*4.* "Other sheep I have which are not of this fold; them also I must bring, and they will hear My voice; and there will be one flock and one shepherd" (John 10:16 NKJV). Thank the Lord that salvation was offered to the Gentiles as well as the Jews. Jesus is speaking here about gathering Gentiles into His flock. "There is neither Jew nor Greek, there is neither slave nor free, there is neither male nor female; for you are all one in Christ Jesus" (Gal. 3:28 NKJV). In the eyes of God, we are all the same. In the body of Christ, we are all one.

*5.* "Let there be real harmony so there won't be divisions in the church. I plead with you to be of one mind, united in thought and purpose (1 Cor. 1:10 NLT). Paul urged his friends back in Corinth to be of one mind. "Finally, all of you should be of one mind, full of sympathy toward each other, loving one another with tender hearts and humble minds" (1 Pet. 3:8 NLT). Peter associates being of one mind with sympathy, love, tenderness, and humility.

*6.* e, d, a, f, b, c

## DAY THREE

*1.* "Who, contrary to hope, in hope believed, so that he became the father of many nations, according to what was spoken" (Rom. 4:18 NKJV). Abraham, contrary to hope—against all the odds, in the face of the impossible—in hope believed. He trusted God and believed in the hope his Lord had placed before him. Abraham believed God would keep His promise.

*2.* "Surely he will never be shaken" (Ps. 112:6 NKJV). The righteous cannot be shaken. Why? "I foresaw the LORD always before my face, for He is at my right hand, that I may not be shaken" (Acts 2:25 NKJV). David couldn't be shaken because he knew the Lord was right by his side. And Timothy was sent by Paul on a mission to the church in Thessalonica. "To establish you and encourage you concerning your faith, that no one should be shaken" (1 Thess. 3:2, 3 NKJV). We want our hope to stand unshaken. Still, there are times when we need a little encouragement. Paul sent Timothy to remind his fellow believers to keep their eyes on the Lord.

*3.* b, e, d, a, f, c

*4.* "This I recall to my mind, therefore I have hope" (Lam. 3:21 NKJV). "Let us hold fast the confession of our hope without wavering, for He who promised is faithful" (Heb. 10:23 NKJV). "Remember therefore how you have received and heard; hold fast and repent" (Rev. 3:3 NKJV). "Behold, I am coming quickly! Hold fast what you have, that no one may take your crown" (Rev. 3:11 NKJV).

*5.* "Christ as a Son over His own house, whose house we are if we hold fast the confidence and the rejoicing of the hope firm to the end" (Heb. 3:6 NKJV). Or as another translation puts it, "If we keep up our courage and remain confident in our hope in Christ" (NLT). In this verse, our hope is equated with confidence and joy. We hold it firmly, right to the end!

*6.* "Therefore, since we are receiving a kingdom which cannot be shaken, let us have grace, by which we may serve God acceptably with reverence and godly fear" (Heb. 12:28 NKJV). We will receive a kingdom that cannot be shaken. And our lives in the meantime should be characterized by grace, reverence, godly fear, service, and acceptability.

## DAY FOUR

*1.* "I beseech you therefore, brethren, by the mercies of God, that you present your bodies a living sacrifice, holy, acceptable to God, which is your reasonable service" (Rom. 12:1 NKJV). Paul tells us that it is only reasonable for us to present ourselves to God. We are to live holy lives. We are to give ourselves over for His use. We are to do what is acceptable in God's eyes.

*2.* "For to you it has been granted on behalf of Christ, not only to believe in Him, but also to suffer for His sake" (Phil. 1:29 NKJV). Many early Christians suffered for Jesus' sake. Paul was among them, and he commended fellow believers for doing the same. "I now rejoice in my sufferings for you, and fill up in my flesh what is lacking in the afflictions of Christ, for the sake of His body, which is the church" (Col. 1:24 NKJV). Now, Paul is telling his friends that he not only suffers for God, but for them! He is willing to suffer, so long as they can know the truth. "Therefore I endure all things for the sake of the elect, that they also may obtain the salvation which is in Christ Jesus with eternal glory" (2 Tim. 2:10 NKJV). Paul endured all things for the sake of those he was trying to reach. His goal was to bring the gospel to people so that they could be saved.

*3.* d, b, e, g, a, f, c

*4.* "I take pleasure in infirmities, in reproaches, in needs, in persecutions, in distresses, for Christ's sake. For when I am weak, then I am strong" (2 Cor. 12:10 NKJV). How astonishing! Paul says that he takes pleasure in all the hard things. That's quite an attitude. But the reason for Paul's perspective follows his list. He's willing because "when I am weak, then I am strong."

*5.* "Christ died for all so that those who live would not continue to live for themselves. He died for them and was raised from the dead so that they would live for him" (2 Cor. 5:15 NCV). Jesus died so that we could live, true. But He did it so that we would live for Him!

*6.* c, g, e, f, a, h, b, d

## DAY FIVE

*1.* Almost every translation takes the literal route, calling hope our anchor. The Message differs by referring to it as an unbreakable spiritual lifeline. The adjectives used to describe this anchoring hope—sure, steadfast, strong, trustworthy, firm, secure, safe, fixed. And to what does it tie us? The Presence behind the veil, the Most Holy Place in heaven, God's inner sanctuary, the inner sanctuary behind the curtain, right into the very presence of God.

*2.* "He who doubts is like a wave of the sea driven and tossed by the wind" (James 1:6 NKJV). Doubt puts us at the mercy of every turn life takes, every moment of panic, every worry and fear. "We should no longer be children, tossed to and fro and carried about with every wind of doctrine, by the trickery of men, in the cunning craftiness of deceitful plotting" (Eph. 4:14 NKJV). Growing in the faith prevents us from being led astray by false teaching.

*3.* "Let us hold fast the confession of our hope without wavering, for He who promised is faithful" (Heb. 10:23

NKJV). The writer of Hebrews tells us to hold fast to hope and not to waver. Why? Because the One who made the promise of hope to us is faithful. He will stick to His word.

*4.* "He did not waver at the promise of God through unbelief, but was strengthened in faith, giving glory to God" (Rom. 4:20 NKJV). One versions says, "His faith did not leave him, and he did not doubt God's promise; his faith filled him with power, and he gave praise to God. He was absolutely sure that God would be able to do what he had promised" (Rom. 4:20, 21 TEV).

*5.* "Create in me a clean heart, O God, and renew a steadfast spirit within me" (Ps. 51:10 NKJV). "My heart is steadfast, O God, my heart is steadfast" (Ps. 57:7 NKJV). "Therefore, my beloved brethren, be steadfast, immovable, always abounding in the work of the Lord" (1 Cor. 15:58 NKJV). "Resist him, steadfast in the faith" (1 Pet. 5:9 NKJV). "We have become partakers of Christ if we hold the beginning of our confidence steadfast to the end" (Heb. 3:14 NKJV).

# LESSON 4

## DAY ONE

*1.* "Faith is the substance of things hoped for, the evidence of things not seen" (Heb. 11:1 NKJV). "We were saved in this hope, but hope that is seen is not hope; for why does one still hope for what he sees? But if we hope for what we do not see, we eagerly wait for it with perseverance" (Rom. 8:24, 25 NKJV). "Love suffers long and is kind; love does not envy; love does not parade itself, is not puffed up; does not behave rudely, does not seek its own, is not provoked, thinks no evil; does not rejoice in iniquity, but rejoices in the truth; bears all things, believes all things, hopes all things, endures all things" (1 Cor. 13:4–7 NKJV).

*2.* "Remembering without ceasing your work of faith, labor of love, and patience of hope" (1 Thess. 1:3 NKJV). There they are! Faith, hope, and love.

*3.* "We heard of your faith in Christ Jesus and of your love for all the saints" (Col. 1:4 NKJV). The Colossians had gained a reputation for faith and love. "We are bound to thank God always for you, brethren, as it is fitting, because your faith grows exceedingly, and the love of every one of you all abounds toward each other" (2 Thess. 1:3 NKJV). Their faith was growing fast, and their love abounded. "Flee also youthful lusts; but pursue righteousness, faith, love, peace with those who call on

the Lord out of a pure heart" (2 Tim. 2:22 NKJV). Pursue, among other things, faith and love.

*4.* f, c, e, b, h, a, g, d

*5.* "But you, O man of God, flee these things and pursue righteousness, godliness, faith, love, patience, gentleness" (1 Tim. 6:11 NKJV). Paul urged Pastor Titus to make sure "that the older men be sober, reverent, temperate, sound in faith, in love, in patience" (Titus 2:2 NKJV). Jesus, in His letter to one of the seven churches, remarks, "I know your works, love, service, faith, and your patience (Rev. 2:19 NKJV). In all three of these verses, we find faith, love, and patience tied together.

*6.* "May the Lord direct your hearts into the love of God and into the patience of Christ" (2 Thess. 3:5 NKJV). Paul's prayer is that God would direct our hearts. And in what direction has He opened the way? Toward love and patience.

## DAY TWO

*1.* "The testing of your faith produces patience. But let patience have its perfect work, that you may be perfect and complete, lacking nothing" (James 1:3, 4 NKJV). Patience comes with maturity. In fact, James says that patience works in our lives to bring us toward completion.

*2.* "Hope deferred makes the heart sick, but when the desire comes, it is a tree of life" (Prov. 13:12 NKJV). While anticipation can be a part of the fun in waiting for something good, when the thing we hope for is constantly postponed, we weary of waiting. It can actually make us feel restless and queasy and anxious—heartsick.

*3.* "For whatever things were written before were written for our learning, that we through the patience and comfort of the Scriptures might have hope" (Rom. 15:4 NKJV). Scripture comforts us along the way and helps us to have patience.

*4.* "In the **presence** of Your **saints** I will **wait** on Your **name**, for it is **good**" (Ps. 52:9 NKJV). "I will **wait** for **You**, O You his **Strength**" (Ps. 59:9 NKJV). "I will **wait** on the LORD . . .And I will **hope** in **Him**" (Is. 8:17 NKJV). "I will **look** to the LORD; I will **wait** for the **God** of my **salvation**; My God will **hear** me" (Mic. 7:7 NKJV).

*5.* "I waited patiently for the LORD; and He inclined to me, and heard my cry" (Ps. 40:1 NKJV). David waited patiently. God responded by listening, and by answering, no doubt. "The ones that fell on the good ground are those who, having heard the word with a noble and good heart, keep it and bear fruit with patience" (Luke 8:15 NKJV). A good heart accepts the Word of God, but it is only with patience that it will begin to bear fruit. "Strengthened with all might, according to His glorious power, for all patience and longsuffering with joy" (Col. 1:11 NKJV). God strengthens us. With His power enabling us, we can be patient. And not just patient—joyfully patient!

*6.* "Be patient, brethren, until the coming of the Lord. See how the farmer waits for the precious fruit of the earth, waiting patiently for it until it receives the early and latter rain. You also be patient. Establish your hearts, for the coming of the Lord is at hand" (James 5:7, 8 NKJV).

## DAY THREE

*1.* Paul says to put on the full armor. The belt of truth, the breastplate of righteousness, our feet geared up with the preparation of the gospel of peace, the shield of faith, the helmet of salvation, and the sword of the Spirit, which is the Word of God.

*2.* Here are the reasons Paul mentions. So that we'll be able to stand against the wiles of the devil. Because we wrestle against invisible spiritual powers. So that we'll be able to stand "in the evil day"—which refers to final judgment kinds of things. So that after all the struggle and battle, we'll still be standing. So that we can quench the fiery darts of the evil one.

*3.* "He put on righteousness as a breastplate, and a helmet of salvation on His head; He put on the garments of vengeance for clothing, and was clad with zeal as a cloak" (Is. 59:17 NKJV). There's overlap between the two lists—the breastplate and helmet are the same. But God has a couple more really cool "accessories" in His getup—garments of vengeance and zeal for a cloak. Impressive!

*4.* "The night is almost gone; the day of salvation will soon be here. So don't live in darkness. Get rid of your evil deeds. Shed them like dirty clothes. Clothe yourselves with the armor of right living, as those who live in the light" (Rom. 13:12 NLT). Paul warns believers that Christ is coming soon, so "cast off the works of darkness" (NKJV). We have no business living as the faithless, who try to hide their sins in the shadows.

*5.* "You have also given me the shield of Your salvation; Your right hand has held me up, Your gentleness has made me great" (Ps. 18:35 NKJV). God gave David salvation, and that served him as a shield. "The LORD is my strength and my shield; my heart trusted in Him, and I am helped; therefore my heart greatly rejoices, and with

my song I will praise Him" (Ps. 28:7 NKJV). God doesn't just give strength. God is David's strength. God doesn't just provide a shield. He is David's shield. "He will shield you with his wings. He will shelter you with his feathers. His faithful promises are your armor and protection" (Ps. 91:4 NLT). The promises of Scripture are our armor. They protect us.

*6.* Okay. You would have filled in your own name in the appropriate places and come out with something like this: "Lucky Me! Who has it as good as Me? I'm saved by God! The Shield who defends Me, the Sword who brings Me triumph. My enemies will come crawling . . .and I'll march on their backs."

## DAY FOUR

*1.* "I looked, and behold, a white cloud, and on the cloud sat One like the Son of Man, having on His head a golden crown" (Rev. 14:14 NKJV). In the end, Jesus shall wear the crown He deserves.

*2.* f, d, a, c, e, g, b

*3.* Here are four different writers of Scripture, and they all tell us about the crown for which we strive. "Everyone who competes for the prize is temperate in all things. Now they do it to obtain a perishable crown, but we for an imperishable crown" (1 Cor. 9:25 NKJV). Paul says it is an imperishable crown. "Blessed is the man who endures temptation; for when he has been approved, he will receive the crown of life which the Lord has promised to those who love Him" (James 1:12 NKJV). James says the crown of life will go to those who endure, who have been approved, and who love Jesus. "When the Chief Shepherd appears, you will receive the crown of glory that does not fade away" (1 Pet. 5:4 NKJV). Peter says that we will receive the crown of glory when Jesus returns. "Do not fear any of those things which you are about to suffer. Indeed, the devil is about to throw some of you into prison, that you may be tested, and you will have tribulation ten days. Be faithful until death, and I will give you the crown of life" (Rev. 2:10 NKJV). John records a letter from Jesus to His followers. He says that at the end of all our sufferings, trials, and tribulations, we will receive the crown of life.

*4.* "For I am not ashamed of the gospel of Christ, for it is the power of God to salvation for everyone who believes" (Rom. 1:16 NKJV). Paul asked people to pray "for me, that utterance may be given to me, that I may open my mouth boldly to make known the mystery of the gospel" (Eph. 6:19 NKJV). "So, affectionately longing for you, we were well pleased to impart to you not only the gospel of God, but also our own lives, because you had become dear to us" (1 Thess. 2:8 NKJV). Paul didn't just shout out warnings on street corners. He spoke to large groups, true, but he also lived among them for many months, worked side by side with them, and developed strong ties of friendship. He cared deeply about them.

*5.* "For though I am absent in the flesh, yet I am with you in spirit, rejoicing to see your good order and the steadfastness of your faith in Christ" (Col. 2:5 NKJV). Paul assures the Colossian church that though he is far away from them, his thoughts are with them. "Therefore, my beloved and longed-for brethren, my joy and crown, so stand fast in the Lord, beloved" (Phil. 4:1 NKJV). What tender terminology—beloved, longed-for, my joy, my crown. He even says beloved twice! "We are your boast as you also are ours, in the day of the Lord Jesus" (2 Cor. 1:14 NKJV).

*6.* "You are the seal of my apostleship in the Lord" (1 Cor. 9:2 NKJV). "You are our epistle written in our hearts, known and read by all men; clearly you are an epistle of Christ, ministered by us, written not with ink but by the Spirit of the living God, not on tablets of stone but on tablets of flesh, that is, of the heart" (2 Cor. 3:2, 3 NKJV). "You are our glory and joy" (1 Thess. 2:20 NKJV).

## DAY FIVE

*1.* "I will hope continually, and will praise You yet more and more" (Ps. 71:14 NKJV). We can hope continually.

*2.* "Be my strong refuge, to which I may resort continually; You have given the commandment to save me, for You are my rock and my fortress" (Ps. 71:3 NKJV). Whenever we have the need, we can turn to the Lord for refuge. David says he did this continually. "Nevertheless I am continually with You; You hold me by my right hand" (Ps. 73:23 NKJV). God is always with us, and He's holding our hand.

*3.* "The LORD will guide you continually, and satisfy your soul in drought, and strengthen your bones; you shall be like a watered garden, and like a spring of water, whose waters do not fail" (Is. 58:11 NKJV).

*4.* b, f, g, a, c, e, d

*5.* "Continue earnestly in prayer, being vigilant in it with thanksgiving" (Col. 4:2 NKJV). "Continue in faith, love, and holiness, with self-control" (1 Tim. 2:15 NKJV). "Let brotherly love continue" (Heb. 13:1 NKJV). "Strengthening the souls of the disciples, exhorting them to continue in the faith, and saying, 'We must through many tribulations enter the kingdom of God'" (Acts 14:22 NKJV). "But you must continue in the things which you have learned and been assured of, knowing from whom you have learned them" (2 Tim. 3:14 NKJV).

*6.* "That he should continue to live eternally, and not see the Pit" (Ps. 49:9 NKJV). Eternal life!

# LESSON 5

## DAY ONE

*1.* "Everything God made is waiting with excitement for God to show his children's glory completely. Everything God made was changed to become useless, not by its own wish but because God wanted it and because all along there was this hope: that everything God made would be set free from ruin to have the freedom and glory that belong to God's children. We know that everything God made has been waiting until now in pain, like a woman ready to give birth" (Rom. 8:19–22 NCV). All of creation is waiting to be released from the curse.

*2.* "I spread out my hands to you; My soul longs for you like a thirsty land" (Ps. 143:6 NKJV). David compares his heart's longing to thirst. "Eagerly waiting for the revelation of our Lord Jesus Christ" (1 Cor. 1:7 NKJV). Paul's mission endeavors were probably spurred on by his sense of urgency, for he fully expected Jesus to return at any time. "As for me, I will see Your face in righteousness; I shall be satisfied when I awake in Your likeness" (Ps. 17:15 NKJV). How did David know this! We, too, will only find complete satisfaction when we reach heaven and see our Savior's face.

*3.* "And there shall be no more curse" (Rev. 22:3 NKJV). The curse of sin will be lifted.

*4.* You see! Everyone was on the same page, right from the start. Jesus said, "You will see the Son of Man sitting at the right hand of the Power, and coming with the clouds of heaven" (Mark 14:62 NKJV). The angels said, "This same Jesus, who was taken up from you into heaven, will so come in like manner as you saw Him go into heaven" (Acts 1:11 NKJV). And Paul laid things out quite clearly, "We who are alive and remain shall be caught up together with them in the clouds to meet the Lord in the air. And thus we shall always be with the Lord" (1 Thess. 4:17 NKJV).

*5.* "Behold, I am coming quickly! Hold fast what you have, that no one may take your crown" (Rev. 3:11 NKJV). "Behold, I am coming quickly! Blessed is he who keeps the words of the prophecy of this book" (Rev. 22:7 NKJV).

"Behold, I am coming quickly, and My reward is with Me, to give to every one according to his work" (Rev. 22:12 NKJV). "He who testifies to these things says, 'Surely I am coming quickly.' Amen. Even so, come, Lord Jesus!" (Rev. 22:20 NKJV).

*6.* "As the days of Noah were, so also will the coming of the Son of Man be" (Matt. 24:37 NKJV). "Be ready, for the Son of Man is coming at an hour you do not expect" (Matt. 24:44 NKJV). "As the lightning comes from the east and flashes to the west, so also will the coming of the Son of Man be" (Matt. 24:27 NKJV). "In the days before the flood, they were eating and drinking, marrying and giving in marriage, until the day Noah entered the ark, and did not know until the flood came and took them all away, so also will the coming of the Son of Man be" (Matt. 24:38, 39 NKJV).

## DAY TWO

*1.* "A man is justified by faith apart from the deeds of the law" (Rom. 3:28 NKJV). We cannot earn our justification by any good deed or adherence to a code of conduct. Our salvation comes by faith. "Having been justified by faith, we have peace with God through our Lord Jesus Christ" (Rom. 5:1 NKJV). "Having now been justified by His blood, we shall be saved from wrath through Him" (Rom. 5:9 NKJV). Justification comes by faith in Jesus, whose sacrifice and blood made it available to us. He is our Source of salvation.

*2.* e, a, d, f, b, g, c

*3.* "Jude, a bondservant of Jesus Christ, and brother of James, to those who are called, sanctified by God the Father, and preserved in Jesus Christ" (Jude 1 NKJV). We are sanctified by God. "Brethren, I commend you to God and to the word of His grace, which is able to build you up and give you an inheritance among all those who are sanctified" (Acts 20:32 NKJV). God sanctifies us through His Word, which is also able to build us up and give us an inheritance. "Therefore if anyone cleanses himself from the latter, he will be a vessel for honor, sanctified and useful for the Master, prepared for every good work (2 Tim. 2:21 NKJV). The believer who is sanctified has made herself ready for her Master's use.

*4.* d, g, e, b, a, h, c, f

*5.* "But when Jesus was glorified, then they remembered that these things were written about Him" (John 12:16 NKJV). Jesus was the first Man to be glorified. He was given a new body, a glorified body. "Whom He predestined, these He also called; whom He called, these He also jus-

tified; and whom He justified, these He also glorified" (Rom. 8:30 NKJV). We will be glorified. "If indeed we suffer with Him, that we may also be glorified together" (Rom. 8:17 NKJV). We share in His death—His sacrifice covers our sins. We will share in His life—we will live forever with Him.

*6.* "Therefore, having been justified by faith, we have peace with God through our Lord Jesus Christ, through whom also we have access by faith into this grace in which we stand, and rejoice in hope of the glory of God" (Rom. 5:1, 2 NKJV).

## DAY THREE

*1.* "Return, O LORD! How long? And have compassion on Your servants" (Ps. 90:13 NKJV). David's longing to be near to God echoes our own eagerness to see Jesus face-to-face. We await His return.

*2.* e, d, g, a, f, b, c

*3.* "A little while, and you will not see Me; and again a little while, and you will see Me" (John 16:19 NKJV). Jesus said it would be just a little while.

*4.* "The Lord isn't really being slow about his promise to return, as some people think. No, he is being patient for your sake. He does not want anyone to perish, so he is giving more time for everyone to repent" (2 Pet. 3:9 NLT). God loves us, and He's merciful to give as many of us the opportunity to come to Him in faith.

*5.* "Even we ourselves groan within ourselves, eagerly waiting for the adoption, the redemption of our body" (Rom. 8:23 NKJV). "But if we hope for what we do not see, we eagerly wait for it with perseverance" (Rom. 8:25 NKJV). ". . .Eagerly waiting for the revelation of our Lord Jesus Christ" (1 Cor. 1:7 NKJV). "We through the Spirit eagerly wait for the hope of righteousness by faith" (Gal. 5:5 NKJV). "Our citizenship is in heaven, from which we also eagerly wait for the Savior, the Lord Jesus Christ" (Phil. 3:20 NKJV). "To those who eagerly wait for Him He will appear a second time, apart from sin, for salvation" (Heb. 9:28 NKJV).

*6.* "Looking for and hastening the coming of the day of God" (2 Pet. 3:12 NKJV). Peter couldn't wait to see Jesus again. They had been good friends, and Peter's heart longed for Him. He not only watched for the coming, he tried to hasten it along!

*7.* "Watch, stand fast in the faith, be brave, be strong" (1 Cor. 16:13 NKJV). We have no idea when the time may come, so we must always be ready. Paul says to watch.

## DAY FOUR

*1.* "While we do not look at the things which are seen, but at the things which are not seen. For the things which are seen are temporary, but the things which are not seen are eternal" (2 Cor. 4:18 NKJV). The eyes of our understanding have been opened, and we know that the spiritual world that wars around us is hidden from our eyes. "Look! I see the heavens opened and the Son of Man standing at the right hand of God" (Acts 7:56 NKJV). As Stephen was dying, the veil was lifted from his eyes, and he saw into heaven. "Look for a new heavens and a new earth in which righteousness dwells" (2 Pet. 3:13 NKJV). Our perspective is unique, and we are looking forward to something far different than others. We are looking forward to the day when we will see our Savior face-to-face, and all things will be made new.

*2.* "We know that when He is revealed, we shall be like Him, for we shall see Him as He is" (1 John 3:2 NKJV). We shall see Jesus, and we shall be made like Him.

*3.* "All flesh shall see the salvation of God." That means everyone! "As I live, says the Lord, Every knee shall bow to Me, And every tongue shall confess to God" (Rom. 14:11 NKJV). In the end, all will be forced to acknowledge Jesus' authority over all creation. "At the name of Jesus every knee should bow, of those in heaven, and of those on earth, and of those under the earth, and that every tongue should confess that Jesus Christ is Lord, to the glory of God the Father" (Phil. 2:10, 11 NKJV).

*4.* "When that which is perfect has come, then that which is in part will be done away. For now we see in a mirror, dimly, but then face to face. Now I know in part, but then I shall know just as I also am known" (1 Cor. 13:10, 12 NKJV).

*5.* "They shall see His face, and His name shall be on their foreheads" (Rev. 22:4 NKJV).

*6.* "I will give him a white stone, and on the stone a new name written which no one knows except him who receives it" (Rev. 2:17 NKJV). The world is full of Marys and Jennifers and Annes. To keep us all sorted out in heaven, we'll each be given our own unique name. A special name that Jesus will call us by.

## DAY FIVE

*1.* "So when this corruptible has put on incorruption, and this mortal has put on immortality, then shall be brought to pass the saying that is written: 'Death is swallowed up in victory' " (1 Cor. 15:54 NKJV).

*2.* "Yea, though I walk through the valley of the shadow of death, I will fear no evil; for You are with me; Your rod and Your staff, they comfort me" (Ps. 23:4 NKJV). Why isn't David afraid? Because, "You are with me." He's not afraid because he's not alone. Neither are we.

*3.* "Release those who through fear of death were all their lifetime subject to bondage" (Heb. 2:15 NKJV). Jesus provided a way to eternal life so that we would have no reason to fear death.

*4.* "We are always confident, knowing that while we are at home in the body we are absent from the Lord. . . . We are confident, yes, well pleased rather to be absent from the body and to be present with the Lord. Therefore we make it our aim, whether present or absent, to be well pleasing to Him" (2 Cor. 5:6, 8, 9 NKJV). When we leave our bodies behind in death, we are in the Lord's presence, according to Paul. He made no bones about admitting that he'd rather be with Jesus, given the choice! But while living, he planned to live in a manner pleasing to the Lord.

*5.* "I have hope in God, which they themselves also accept, that there will be a resurrection of the dead, both of the just and the unjust" (Acts 24:15 NKJV). There will be a resurrection. "I do not want you to be ignorant, brethren, concerning those who have fallen asleep, lest you sorrow as others who have no hope. For if we believe that Jesus died and rose again, even so God will bring with Him those who sleep in Jesus" (1 Thess. 4:13, 14 NKJV).

*6.* No more death. No more sorrow. No more crying. No more pain.

# LESSON 6

## DAY ONE

*1.* "Hope in God" (NKJV). When you're feeling down, getting discouraged, feeling sad or upset—that's the time to hang on to hope. "I will put my hope in God" (Ps. 42:5 NLT). "I fix my eyes on God" (MSG).

*2.* c, e, a, d, b

*3.* "Surely there is a hereafter, and your hope will not be cut off" (Prov. 23:18 NKJV). We can rest in this knowledge. "For I know the thoughts that I think toward you, says the LORD, thoughts of peace and not of evil, to give you a future and a hope" (Jer. 29:11 NKJV). God has a hope for us—a hope and a future. This is a comfort when we hit rough patches.

*4.* "Perseverance, character, and character; hope" (Rom. 5:4 NKJV). Endurance, perseverance—they build character. Character strengthens our hope. "So let it grow, for when your endurance is fully developed, you will be strong in character and ready for anything" (NLT). With strength of character and hope, we will be ready to face anything life might throw our way.

*5.* We are to "show the same diligence" (NKJV). We are to "go on with the same hard work" all our lives (NCV). We are to "keep right on" for "as long as life lasts" (NLT). And we must "extend that same intensity toward a full-bodied hope" (MSG). (Heb. 6:10–12).

*6.* "For he will not dwell unduly on the days of his life, because God keeps him busy with the joy of his heart" (Eccl. 5:20 NKJV). We're not trapped in the boredom of a waiting room. God keeps us busy. We have a life to live, filled with joy from our Heavenly Father.

## DAY TWO

*1.* "Therefore know this day, and consider it in your heart, that the LORD Himself is God in heaven above and on the earth beneath; there is no other" (Deut. 4:39 NKJV). "I know that whatever God does, it shall be forever. Nothing can be added to it, and nothing taken from it. God does it, that men should fear before Him" (Eccl 3:14 NKJV). "We have come to believe and know that You are the Christ, the Son of the living God" (John 6:69 NKJV). I couldn't say it any better!

*2.* f, d, b, c, g, e, a

*3.* "I will give them a heart to know Me, that I am the LORD; and they shall be My people, and I will be their God, for they shall return to Me with their whole heart" (Jer. 24:7 NKJV). "The people who know their God shall be strong, and carry out great exploits" (Dan. 11:32 NKJV). "We know that all things work together for good to those who love God, to those who are the called according to His purpose" (Rom. 8:28 NKJV). "Now we have received . . .the Spirit who is from God, that we might know the things that have been freely given to us by God" (1 Cor. 2:12 NKJV).

*4.* "Sanctify the Lord God in your hearts, and always be ready to give a defense to everyone who asks you a reason for the hope that is in you, with meekness and fear" (1 Pet. 3:15 NKJV). You need to know it well enough to explain it to someone who asks you about it.

*5.* c, a, e, b, d

*6.* "Now, Lord, look on their threats, and grant to Your servants that with all boldness they may speak Your word. . . . And when they had prayed, the place where they were assembled together was shaken; and they were all filled with the Holy Spirit, and they spoke the word of God with boldness" (Acts 4:29, 31 NKJV). Our boldness comes as an answer to prayer and through the Holy Spirit's working. "And for me, that utterance may be given to me, that I may open my mouth boldly to make known the mystery of the gospel, for which I am an ambassador in chains; that in it I may speak boldly, as I ought to speak" (Eph. 6:19, 20 NKJV).

## DAY THREE

*1.* "But God, who is rich in mercy, because of His great love with which He loved us. . ." (Eph. 2:4 NKJV). God is rich in mercy, and He has a great love for us. "Now may our Lord Jesus Christ Himself, and our God and Father, who has loved us and given us everlasting consolation and good hope by grace" (2 Thess. 2:16 NKJV). God has given us His love and an everlasting hope. "In this is love, not that we loved God, but that He loved us and sent His Son to be the propitiation for our sins" (1 John 4:10 NKJV). We couldn't have loved God if He had not first loved us.

*2.* "He chose us in Him before the foundation of the world, that we should be holy and without blame before Him in love" (Eph. 1:4 NKJV). "[He] has saved us and called us with a holy calling, not according to our works, but according to His own purpose and grace which was given to us in Christ Jesus before time began" (2 Tim. 1:9 NKJV).

*3.* "Likewise the Spirit also helps in our weaknesses. For we do not know what we should pray for as we ought, but the Spirit Himself makes intercession for us with groanings which cannot be uttered" (Rom. 8:26 NKJV).

*4.* "I do not pray for these alone, but also for those who will believe in Me through their word" (John 17:20 NKJV). Jesus included all who would hear the message of salvation and believe in His prayer. That means you and me, sister!

*5.* "Finally, brethren, pray for us, that the word of the Lord may run swiftly and be glorified, just as it is with you" (2 Thess. 3:1 NKJV). Have you ever thought of this? We can pray that God's Word will reach others for salvation.

*6.* "For this reason we, since the day we heard it, do not cease to pray for you, and to ask that you may be filled with the knowledge of His will in all wisdom and spiritual understanding; that you may walk worthy of the Lord, fully pleasing Him, being fruitful in every good work and increasing in the knowledge of God; strengthened with all might, according to His glorious power, for all patience and longsuffering with joy; giving thanks to the Father" (Col. 1:9–12 NKJV).

## Day Four

*1.* "Let us be glad and rejoice and give Him glory, for the marriage of the Lamb has come, and His wife has made herself ready" (Rev. 19:7 NKJV). All believers will celebrate at the marriage supper of the Lamb. In this verse, gladness and rejoicing are taking place because the bride has made herself ready for her Groom.

*2.* d, a, f, c, e, b

*3.* "I will greatly rejoice in the LORD, My soul shall be joyful in my God; for He has clothed me with the garments of salvation, He has covered me with a robe of righteousness, as a bridegroom decks himself with ornaments, and as a bride adorns herself with jewels" (Is. 61:10 NKJV). Our beautiful "clothes" are salvation and righteousness.

*4.* "Since you have purified your souls in obeying the truth through the Spirit in sincere love of the brethren, love one another fervently with a pure heart" (1 Pet. 1:22 NKJV). Obedience, love, and the working of the Holy Spirit.

*5.* "Your testimonies are very sure; holiness adorns Your house, O LORD, forever" (Ps. 93:5 NKJV). The things of God are adorned with holiness. Our lives should be too! "I adorned you with ornaments, put bracelets on your wrists, and a chain on your neck. . . .Thus you were adorned with gold and silver, and your clothing was of fine linen, silk, and embroidered cloth. You ate pastry of fine flour, honey, and oil. You were exceedingly beautiful, and succeeded to royalty" (Ezek. 16:11, 13 NKJV). God knew all about the pretty things women love. "For in this manner, in former times, the holy women who trusted in God also adorned themselves, being submissive to their own husbands" (1 Pet. 3:5 NKJV). Oh, I know how much that makes some women cringe, but face it, ladies. A woman who is a proper helpmate to her husband is more lovely than the most glamorous supermodel. God says so!

*6.* "Eye has not seen, nor ear heard, Nor have entered into the heart of man the things God has prepared for those who love Him" (1 Cor. 2:9 NKJV). Imagine the most beautiful thing, and heaven will be more beautiful still. Imagine the most awe-inspiring sights, and heaven will leave us even more awestruck. No human being could even imagine the things God has prepared for those who love Him.

## Day Five

*1.* "When I think of the wisdom and scope of God's plan, I fall to my knees and pray to the Father" (Eph. 3:14 NLT).

*2.* "Aspire to lead a quiet life, to mind your own business, and to work with your own hands, as we commanded you" (1 Thess. 4:11 NKJV). God has given you responsibilities. You should aspire to see to them to the best of your ability. Don't go out looking for something more exciting to do. Don't worry about the business that the Lord has given someone else to do. And when another season of life brings new opportunities your way, trust God to lead you in taking on new and different responsibilities.

*3.* "I know whom I have believed and am persuaded that He is able to keep what I have committed to Him until that Day" (2 Tim. 1:12 NKJV). Not only does Paul say that he knows Jesus, he says he's sure that Jesus will be able to fulfill all His promises in the end.

*4.* f, b, d, g, a, e, h, c

*5.* "Watch therefore, for you know neither the day nor the hour in which the Son of Man is coming" (Matt. 25:13 NKJV). "Take heed, watch and pray; for you do not know when the time is" (Mark 13:33 NKJV). "Watch therefore, for you do not know when the master of the house is coming—in the evening, at midnight, at the crowing of the rooster, or in the morning" (Mark 13:35 NKJV). "Therefore let us not sleep, as others do, but let us watch and be sober" (1 Thess. 5:6 NKJV).

*6.* "O Israel, hope in the LORD from this time forth and forever" (Ps. 131:3 NKJV). We can hope in the Lord forever. He will never disappoint us. "Live in such a way that God's love can bless you as you wait for the eternal life that our Lord Jesus Christ in his mercy is going to give you" (Jude 21 NLT). While we're waiting for our hopes to come to reality, we can live in a way that pleases God. His love blesses us. "Blessed are those servants whom the master, when he comes, will find watching. Assuredly, I say to you that he will gird himself and have them sit down to eat, and will come and serve them" (Luke 12:37 NKJV). How truly blessed we will be if we are found faithful when Jesus comes.

**WOMEN OF FAITH®**
A Division of Thomas Nelson, Inc.

**PRESENTS**

# Irrepressible
# HOPE
CONFERENCE 2004

## Featured Speakers & Dramatist:

Sheila Walsh

Marilyn Meberg

Luci Swindoll

Patsy Clairmont

Thelma Wells

Nicole Johnson

*There is more to life than just staying afloat!*
Experience the all-new two day conference that can put fresh wind in your sails — with stirring music, engaging dramatic presentations and refreshing messages.

*We have this hope as an anchor for the soul, firm and secure.*
—HEBREWS 6:19

## 2004 Event Cities and Special Guests

**Shreveport, LA**
February 27-28
CenturyTel Center

**Philadelphia, PA - I**
March 5-6
Wachovia Spectrum

**San Antonio, TX***
**March 18-20**
**AlamoDome**

**Ft. Wayne, IN**
March 26-27
Allen County
War Memorial
Coliseum- Arena

**Spokane, WA**
April 16-17
Spokane Arena

**Cincinnati, OH**
April 23-24
US Bank Arena

**San Jose, CA**
May 7-8
HP Pavilion

**Nashville, TN**
May 14-15
Gaylord Entertainment
Center

**Charleston, SC**
May 21-22
N. Charleston Coliseum

**Des Moines, IA**
June 4-5
Veterans Memorial
Auditorium

**Anaheim, CA - I**
June 18-19
Arrowhead Pond

**Pittsburgh, PA**
June 25-26
Mellon Arena

**Denver, CO**
July 9-10
Pepsi Center

**Ft. Lauderdale, FL**
July 16-17
Office Depot Center

**St. Louis, MO**
July 23-24
Savvis Center

**Atlanta, GA**
July 30-31
Philips Arena

**Washington, DC**
August 6-7
MCI Center

**Buffalo, NY**
August 13-14
HSBC Arena

**Omaha, NE**
August 20-21
Qwest Center Omaha

**Dallas, TX**
August 27-28
American Airlines Center

**Anaheim, CA - II**
September 10-11
Arrowhead Pond

**Albany, NY**
September 17-18
Pepsi Arena

**Philadelphia, PA - II**
September 24-25
Wachovia Center

**Hartford, CT**
October 1-2
Hartford Civic Center

**Portland, OR**
October 8-9
Rose Garden Arena

**Orlando, FL**
October 15-16
TD Waterhouse Centre

**St. Paul, MN**
October 22-23
Xcel Energy Center

**Charlotte, NC**
October 29-30
Charlotte Coliseum

**Oklahoma City, OK**
November 5-6
Ford Center

**Vancouver, BC**
November 12-13
GM Place

*Dates and locations subject to change.*

***Special National Conference. Call 1-888-49-FAITH for details.***

For more information call **1-888-49-FAITH** or visit **womenoffaith.com**

# The Complete Women of Faith®
## Study Guide Series

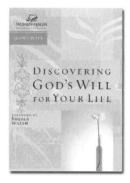

Discovering God's
Will for Your Life
0-7852-4983-4

Living Above
Worry and Stress
0-7852-4986-9

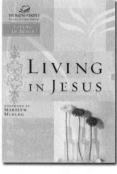

Living in Jesus
0-7852-4985-0

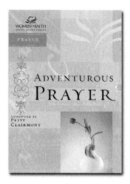

Adventurous
Prayer
0-7852-4984-2

## NEW RELEASES

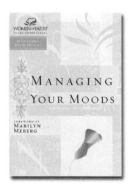

Managing
Your Moods
0-7852-5151-0

Cultivating
Contentment
0-7852-5152-9

Encouraging
One Another
0-7852-5153-7

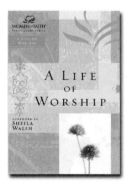

A Life of Worship
0-7852-5154-5

WOMEN OF FAITH®

# A Message of Grace & Hope for Every Day

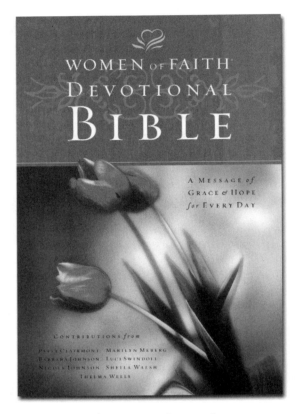

Hardcover: 0-7180-0378-0
Paperback: 0-7180-0377-2
Bonded Leather: 0-7180-0379-9

The *Women of Faith® Devotional Bible* provides women with the inspiration and resources needed to strengthen their walk with God and build stronger relationships with others. It helps women of all ages and stages in life — mature believers and those who have yet to believe, from all backgrounds, church and non-churched — to grow spiritually, emotionally, and relationally.